Grammar Practice

Grade 12

Dashes
Spelling Prepositions
Mood
Places
Verb Clause Nouns
Adjective Case Predicate
Active Prefixes
Misplaced Adverb
Suffixes Purpose
Nominative Phrases
Gerunds Commas
Double Verbs Verbals
Tense Dangling
Noun Pronoun Superlative
Colons People
Sentence Negative
Series Voice Agreement Passive
Italics Forms Plurals

Table of Contents

MODULE 1: PARTS OF SPEECH
NOUNS

The Eight Parts of Speech			
noun	adjective	pronoun	conjunction
verb	adverb	preposition	interjection

1a   A *noun* is a word used to name a person, a place, a thing, or an idea.

PERSONS	janitor, Dorothea Dix, aunt, rock star, friend
PLACES	Dallas, Idaho, station, park, cafeteria, lake
THINGS	orange, modem, illness, orchid, insects
IDEAS	education, ambition, theory, courage, democracy

1b   A *common noun* names any one of a group of persons, places, things, or ideas. A *proper noun* names a particular person, place, thing, or idea.

COMMON NOUNS	man, state, event, holiday, language, vehicle, street, building
PROPER NOUNS	Thomas Jefferson, Texas, Winter Olympics, Groundhog Day, Swahili, Toyota Prius, Pennsylvania Avenue, Museum of Modern Art

1c   A *concrete noun* names an object that can be perceived by the senses (hearing, sight, smell, taste, and touch). An *abstract noun* names a quality, characteristic, or idea.

CONCRETE NOUNS	Mexico City, sidewalk, teakettle, President Lincoln, toucan, wombat, light, heat
ABSTRACT NOUNS	truth, gratefulness, belief, bravery, attitude, fate, democracy, wit

1d   A *collective noun* names a group.

EXAMPLES   herd, troop, congress, pack, jury

1e   A *compound noun* consists of two or more words used together as a single noun. Some compound nouns are written as one word, some as separate words, and others as hyphenated words.

EXAMPLES   boardwalk, Ferris wheel, editor-at-large

EXERCISE 1   Classifying Nouns

Classify each noun below. First, write *C* for *common* or *P* for *proper*. Then, if the noun is *compound,* write *COMP,* and if it is *collective,* write *COLL.* Use a semicolon to separate your answers.

EX.   _C; COLL_   family

_____ 1. happiness   _____ 9. Mount Everest

_____ 2. council   _____ 10. roller coaster

_____ 3. Emma Watson   _____ 11. flock

_____ 4. parking lot   _____ 12. California

_____ 5. doubt   _____ 13. sketchbook

_____ 6. Dev Patel   _____ 14. father-in-law

_____ 7. team   _____ 15. cello

_____ 8. blackberry

EXERCISE 2   Classifying Concrete Nouns and Abstract Nouns

Classify each italicized noun. Then write *C* if the noun is concrete or *A* if it is abstract. Use a semicolon to separate your answers.

EX.   _C; A_   *Enrico* never misses his karate *lesson.*

_____ 1. *Yolanda* put on her elbow-length *gloves.*

_____ 2. The *sunset* tonight is an amazing *purple.*

_____ 3. Jorge has nothing but *impatience* for junk *mail.*

_____ 4. *Oprah Winfrey* shows great *talent* as an interviewer.

_____ 5. My *family* eats a great deal of *soup* in the *winter.*

_____ 6. The store *motto* is "satisfaction guaranteed."

_____ 7. Serena dropped her *phone* in a puddle, but it still worked when *Mom* used it.

_____ 8. "Do not trade *justice* for economy," the *speaker* urged.

_____ 9. I love the type of *pottery* with the cracked *finish.*

_____ 10. She hasn't any *tact,* but she makes up for it with her *humor.*

_____ 11. The *confidence* of the *runner* inspired us.

_____ 12. *Joel* called his mother after the *game.*

_____ 13. At *school,* we discussed unconscious *biases.*

_____ 14. My *house* is a historical *landmark.*

_____ 15. Many people have great *respect* for Edmonia Lewis's *sculpture.*

MODULE 1: PARTS OF SPEECH
PRONOUNS

1f   A *pronoun* is a word used in place of a noun or more than one noun.

Personal Pronouns	I, me, my, mine, we, us, our, ours, you, your, yours, he, him, his, she, her, hers, it, its, they, them, their, theirs
Relative Pronouns	that, which, who, whom, whose
Interrogative Pronouns	who, whose, what, whom, which
Demonstrative Pronouns	this, that, these, those
Indefinite Pronouns	all, another, any, anybody, anyone, anything, both, each, either, everybody, everyone, everything, few, many, more, most, much, neither, nobody, none, no one, one, other, several, some, somebody, someone, something, such
Reflexive and Intensive Pronouns	myself, ourselves, yourself, yourselves, himself, herself, itself, themselves

NOTE   In this module, words such as *my*, *your*, *his*, *hers*, *ours*, and *theirs* are treated as possessive pronouns rather than as adjectives. Follow your teacher's guidelines when referring to such words.

The word that a pronoun stands for is called its ***antecedent***. A pronoun may appear in the same sentence as its antecedent or in a following sentence. The antecedent may be a noun or another pronoun.

EXAMPLES   **Latoya** loves her **cat**. **She** takes good care of **it**. [*Latoya* is the antecedent of *she*. *Cat* is the antecedent of *it*.]

We told **her** that **she** could stay with **us**. [*We* is the antecedent of *us*. *Her* is the antecedent of *she*.]

EXERCISE 3   Identifying Pronouns

Underline the pronoun in each sentence below.

EX.   <u>Which</u> of the hats did Alfred choose?

1. Try to be yourself during the interview.

2. Everyone wanted to get tickets to the concert.

3. Jake always knocks too hard on our door.

4. Math is the class that follows gym.

5. Clea sang a song nobody else knew.

6. The writer himself couldn't understand the book.

7. Before the hike, Sally and Mia tightened the laces on their boots.

8. Divers collected many of the specimens out near the reef.

9. My sister has always wanted to be in the Olympics.

10. The server told Henry that he liked the garden salad.

11. Who is available to help move the sofa?

12. Aunt Phyllis took me to the beach last summer.

13. We walked silently up the hill and into the woods.

14. Carlos is the neighbor who found the cat in the bushes.

15. These are the mittens made in Norway.

EXERCISE 4   Identifying Pronouns and Their Antecedents

Underline the pronouns in the paragraph below. Then double underline the antecedent of each pronoun.

EX.   <u>Louis Braille</u> dedicated <u>his</u> life to helping people with visual impairments.

[1] The son of a saddlemaker, Louis Braille blinded himself in an accident at the age of three. [2] At the time, the accident seemed tragic, yet it set in motion an extraordinary life and career. [3] Braille went to Paris to attend a school that taught visually impaired people to read using raised letters. [4] However, this was a very

slow method for reading a whole book. [5] Then Braille met a visually impaired concert pianist who paid for him to learn to play the church organ. [6] Eventually, Braille earned his reputation as a talented organist, and good fortune followed. [7] But the young man had taken a vow to help visually impaired people, and he never forgot it. [8] Using money that he made playing the organ, Braille worked for years on his ideas to help others like himself. [9] The result was the Braille reading system, into which both numbers and letters can be translated. [10] If Louis Braille had never lost his sight, perhaps most people who are blind would still be unable to read for themselves.

ADJECTIVES

1g   An *adjective* is a word used to modify a noun or pronoun.

To *modify* means "to describe or to make more definite." Adjectives modify nouns or pronouns by telling *what kind*, *which one*, or *how many (how much)*.

What kind?	**helpful** librarian, **cool** breeze
Which one?	**that** star, **final** exam, **next** day
How much?	**more** work, **two** steps, **less** time

The words *a*, *an*, and *the* also modify nouns. These words are called **articles**.

A and *an* are **indefinite articles**. They refer to any one of a general group. *A* is used before words beginning with a consonant sound; *an* is used before words beginning with a vowel sound. *An* is used before words beginning with the consonant *h* when the *h* is not pronounced.

EXAMPLES   Pressed between the pages of the book was **a** single rose petal.
            We saw **an** interesting film about African history.
            Having dinner with the president is **an** honor.

The is the **definite article**. It refers to a particular person, place, thing, or idea.

EXAMPLE   **The** last song of **the** evening was a slow, sad one.

Sometimes nouns are used as adjectives.

EXAMPLES   What caused the **train** wreck? [*Train,* usually a noun, is used as an adjective to modify the noun *wreck.*]
            The **restaurant** manager donates food to a local shelter. [*Restaurant,* usually a noun, is used as an adjective to modify the noun *manager.*]

NOTE   Some pairs or groups of nouns are considered compound nouns. By checking a dictionary, you can avoid confusing a noun that is used as an adjective with a noun that is part of a compound noun.

    COMPOUND NOUNS   space station, soy sauce, goose egg, Mexico City

NOTE   Possessive forms of nouns are not considered adjectives, even though they modify nouns and pronouns.

    POSSESSIVE NOUNS   I enjoyed reading **Alyssa's** story.

EXERCISE 5   Identifying Adjectives in Sentences

Underline the adjectives in each sentence below, and double underline the word or words each adjective modifies. Do not include *a*, *an*, or *the*.

EX.   The Polos set out for China in 1271 to visit the <u>Mongol</u> <u><u>emperor</u></u>, Kublai Khan.

1. Their long journey took them over vast deserts.

2. The Polo brothers, Niccolò and Maffeo, were Venetian merchants, and Marco was Niccolò's son.

3. The Polos were bringing holy oil from Jerusalem to Kublai Khan.

4. They traveled through the Pamir Mountains, which had higher peaks than any other mountains they crossed.

5. At night, they used the stars to tell them the correct direction to head.

6. That trip brought the Polos to wondrous places.

7. The Polos spent a year in Campichu, a grand city full of golden statues.

8. Marco Polo described the Gobi Desert as having sandy hills and valleys and containing no food at all.

9. In 1275, the Polos arrived at the Khan's summer palace in the eastern city of Shangtu.

10. Their historic journey had taken over three years.

11. Kublai Khan employed Marco Polo as a foreign official of the Asian empire.

12. On one trip, Marco went to Yunnan province.

13. As a traveling official, Marco was expected to be a keen and truthful observer.

14. Later, he told incredible tales about China.

15. A curious writer, Rustichello, made Marco's travels famous in a book, *Description of the World*.

MODULE 1: PARTS OF SPEECH
VERBS

1h   A *verb* is a word that expresses action or a state of being.

(1) An *action verb* expresses physical or mental activity.

EXAMPLES   shriek, think, hope, break, growl, forget, jog, try, laugh, buy

(2) A *transitive verb* is an action verb that takes an *object*—a noun or pronoun that tells *who* or *what* receives the action of the verb.

EXAMPLES   The cat **emptied** its water bowl. [*Water bowl* receives the action of the verb *emptied*.]
The thunder **rattled** the windows. [*Windows* receive the action of the verb *rattled*.]

(3) An *intransitive verb* is an action verb that does not take an object.

EXAMPLES   Lena's balloon **sailed** away.
An osprey **soared** over the treetops.

A verb can be transitive in one sentence and intransitive in another.

EXAMPLES   You really **burst** my bubble. [transitive]
The dam **burst**. [intransitive]

(4) A *linking verb,* or *state-of-being verb,* connects the subject with a noun, a pronoun, or an adjective that identifies or describes it.

The most commonly used linking verbs are forms of the verb *be*: *am, is, are, was, were, being, been,* and so on. Other common linking verbs include *appear, become, feel, grow, look, remain, seem, smell, sound, stay, taste,* and *turn.*

EXAMPLES   Amelia **is** the captain of the team.
The night **grew** cold and spooky.

Many linking verbs can be used as action verbs as well.

EXAMPLES   This milk **has turned** sour. [The verb links the subject, *milk*, to a word that describes it, *sour*.]
A police car **turned** the corner. [The verb describes an action taken by the subject, *police car*.]

(5) A *verb phrase* consists of a *main verb* and at least one *helping*, or *auxiliary*, verb. Common helping verbs are forms of *be*, forms of *have*, forms of *do*, and the auxiliaries *can, could, may, might, must, shall, should, will*, and *would*.

EXAMPLES   **does** know, **must have been** hurrying, **is** now sailing

EXERCISE 6   Identifying Transitive and Intransitive Verbs

In the sentences below, identify each italicized verb as transitive or intransitive. Write *T* for *transitive* or *I* for *intransitive* on the line before each sentence.

EX. ___*I*___ The crew *calmed* down after the storm.

_____ 1. The chef *cooked* all night.

_____ 2. We *turned* the dial to the public radio station.

_____ 3. Whom *did* you *elect* treasurer?

_____ 4. Marjorie *flipped* the pancakes like an expert.

_____ 5. Toshiro *wrote* frequently to his uncle.

_____ 6. Please *send* Stamos my best wishes.

_____ 7. The receiver *looked* over his shoulder as he ran.

_____ 8. Yesterday Grace *bowled* a perfect game.

_____ 9. Two coats of paint *work* better than one.

_____ 10. Which hamster *crawled* into your glove?

EXERCISE 7   Identifying Verb Phrases and Helping Verbs

In each sentence, underline the verb phrase once and the helping verb(s), twice.

EX.   Do you play the piano?

1. George will be the first one at the planetarium.
2. That tree was transplanted here from another part of the country.
3. May I go to Chelsea's house?
4. I can remember it perfectly.
5. The senators are debating the issue right this minute.
6. Sondra had always helped her mother make desserts.
7. His package might have been sent to the wrong address.
8. Does Yolanda usually ride this bus?
9. Our project should definitely win a prize at the science fair.
10. Miguel is thinking about tomorrow's trip.

MODULE 1: PARTS OF SPEECH

ADVERBS

1i An *adverb* is a word used to modify a verb, an adjective, another adverb, or an entire clause or sentence.

Adverbs modify by telling *how*, *when*, *where*, or *to what extent*.

How?	Todd washed the car **quickly**. Marissa works **fast**.
When?	The patient is resting **now**. Winter came **early** last year.
Where?	May we look **around**? Please come **here**.
To what extent?	We **almost** had an accident. The weather was **extremely** bad.

EXAMPLES   After the operation, Mr. Santos could see **clearly** again. [*Clearly* modifies the verb, telling *how* Mr. Santos *could see.*]

The lions were **quite** hungry. [*Quite* modifies the adjective, telling *to what extent* the lions were *hungry.*]

Chandra dances **more** gracefully than I. [*More* modifies the adverb, telling *to what extent* Chandra dances *gracefully.*]

EXERCISE 8   Identifying Adverbs and the Words They Modify

Underline the adverbs in each sentence. Draw brackets around the word(s) that each adverb modifies. Then identify the modified word(s) by writing *V* for *verb*, *ADJ* for *adjective*, or *ADV* for *adverb*.

EX. __*V*__   Giselle [returned] today.

_____ 1. Every morning, he quickly turned off the alarm.

_____ 2. Completely happy with the show, the critic wrote a good review.

_____ 3. The building was later finished.

_____ 4. Some sports figures are extremely talented.

_____ 5. Our teacher often likes to tell about her trip to Mexico.

_____ 6. Park the truck closer to the entrance.

_____ 7. Jewel wondered if she would ever get to see Dallas.

_____ 8. To open the door, push the lever forward.

_____ 9. Happily, the three of them ran to the park.

_____ 10. Fred claimed he had found a new job accidentally.

_____ 11. Hector ran immediately to aid his brother.

_____ 12. The people next door just recently moved in.

_____ 13. I consider myself quite lucky to have been chosen.

_____ 14. Several of the most popular games were played at the party.

_____ 15. Enthusiastically, Melba introduced me to her puppy.

EXERCISE 9   Using Adverbs

Complete each sentence below by supplying an appropriate adverb. The word or phrase in parentheses tells you what information the adverb should give.

EX.   She worked (_How?_) at her new job.
       She worked hard at her new job.

1.   Chad could spell long words (_To what extent?_) well.

    _____

2.   The quarterback threw the pass (_How?_).

    _____

3.   Five of our new computers are kept (_Where?_) in the math room.

    _____

4.   People who wish to run in marathons should practice (_How?_).

    _____

5.   We'll find out the answer (_When?_).

    _____

MODULE 1: PARTS OF SPEECH
REVIEW EXERCISE 1

A.   Classifying Nouns

On the line before each sentence, classify the italicized noun. Write *C* for *concrete* or *A* for *abstract*. Then, if the noun is compound, write *COMP*, and if it is collective, write *COLL*. Use a semicolon to separate your answers.

EX. *C; COMP*   The real *Mother Goose* may have lived in Boston.

_____ 1. There is *evidence* that she was not a kindly bird in a bonnet.

_____ 2. A woman named Elizabeth Foster married *Isaac Goose* in 1682.

_____ 3. Elizabeth's ten new stepchildren made for an unusual *wedding gift*.

_____ 4. She eventually added six of her own children to the *family*.

_____ 5. Elizabeth had a wonderful *memory* for stories, rhymes, and fables.

_____ 6. Thomas Fleet, Mrs. Goose's *son-in-law*, collected and printed some of her tales.

_____ 7. By *tradition*, Mother Goose rhymes have no known author.

_____ 8. Copies of Fleet's *collection* have all disapeared.

_____ 9. Some childhood *favorites*, such as "Old King Cole," are from a French collector.

_____ 10. Elizabeth Goose was buried in a *graveyard* near the Park Street Church.

B.   Classifying Verbs

On the line before each sentence, identify the italicized verb as an action verb or a linking verb. If it is an action verb, tell whether it is transitive or intransitive. Write *AV* for *action verb*, *LV* for *linking verb*, *T* for *transitive*, and *I* for *intransitive*. Use a semicolon to separate your answers.

EX. *AV; T*   Eloise *grew* miniature roses in her window box.

_____ 1. Your brother *looks* taller this year.

_____ 2. That airplane can *fly* faster than any other ever built.

_____ 3. Please *stand* those boxes up in the corner.

_____ 4. Hoy *considered* all his options before deciding.

_____ 5. Only 10 loyal fans *remained* at the end of the game.

_____ 6. Eat your oatmeal before it *gets* cold.

_____ 7. I have *been* so busy, I haven't had time to call.

_____ 8. *Can* we *see* you tomorrow?

_____ 9. The balloon touched the lightbulb and *exploded*.

_____ 10. It *might be* better if we leave early.

C.   Identifying Adjectives and Adverbs

On the line before each sentence, identify the italicized word by writing *ADJ* for *adjective* or *ADV* for *adverb*. Then underline the word or words that the adjective or adverb modifies.

EX. _*ADJ*_   The prow of the ship cut through the *thick* <u>ice</u>.

_____ 1. Everyone was *formally* dressed for the wedding.

_____ 2. I have heard that crocodiles are more *dangerous* than alligators.

_____ 3. The *all-American* hamburger most likely originated in Germany.

_____ 4. Ricardo explained the topic *clearly*.

_____ 5. The settlers stopped to repair the *wagon* wheel.

_____ 6. Remind me *later* to fix that window.

_____ 7. On the way to Boston, we stopped to see the *most* wonderful museum.

_____ 8. The *famous* author spoke at our school.

_____ 9. My cousin has always wanted to be an *airline* pilot.

_____ 10. Wiggins was six-foot-four, so we had to look *up* when we talked to him.

MODULE 1: PARTS OF SPEECH

PREPOSITIONS

1j A *preposition* is a word used to show how a noun or a pronoun is related to some other word in the sentence.

A preposition introduces a *prepositional phrase*. The noun or pronoun that ends a prepositional phrase is the *object of the preposition*. In the following examples, the object of the prepositions is *tree*.

Notice how changing the preposition changes the relationship between *flew* and *tree*.

EXAMPLES The bird flew **above** the tree.   The bird flew **beneath** the tree.
The bird flew **into** the tree.   The bird flew **near** the tree.
The bird flew **around** the tree.   The bird flew **toward** the tree.

Commonly Used Prepositions				
aboard	before	by	like	through
about	behind	concerning	near	to
above	below	down	of	toward
across	beneath	during	off	under
after	beside	except	on	until
against	besides	for	onto	up
along	between	from	outside	upon
among	beyond	in	over	with
around	but (meaning	inside	past	within
at	*except*)	into	since	without

Prepositions may also be compound.

Compound Prepositions			
according to	because of	in place of	next to
along with	by means of	in spite of	on account of
as of	in addition to	instead of	out of

NOTE Some words may be either an adverb or a preposition, depending on their use in a sentence.

EXAMPLES During the storm, please stay **inside**. [adverb]
The parrot was sleeping **inside** his cage. [preposition]

EXERCISE 10   Identifying Prepositions and Their Objects

Underline each preposition in the sentences below. Draw a bracket around its object. A sentence may contain more than one preposition.

EX.   Samuel lives <u>near</u> the [lake].

1. Have you ever heard the song "Over the Rainbow"?
2. I've had the same backpack for two years.
3. My aunt does not allow phones at the dinner table.
4. The meteorologist reported that we could expect more sunshine in the afternoon.
5. Finding a parking place near that theater can often be difficult.
6. I tried reasoning with him, but he wouldn't listen to me.
7. If she's not here by noon, send her a text.
8. We were thrilled that our team won against all odds.
9. I wore a jacket instead of a sweater.
10. Do you think life exists outside our solar system?

EXERCISE 11   Writing an Explanation of Services

You and some friends have started making food for parties in the neighborhood. The Community Service Bureau keeps a register of various businesses in the community. The bureau will list your business if you write a short explanation of your services. Write 10 sentences explaining the kind of food you cook and how it's presented. Underline at least five prepositional phrases and include at least three compound prepositions.

EX.   *Our business offers a menu <u>with many different options</u>.*

_____

_____

_____

_____

_____

_____

_____

_____

_____

_____

CONJUNCTIONS AND INTERJECTIONS

1k A *conjunction* is a word used to join words or groups of words.

(1) A *coordinating conjunction* connects words or groups of words that are used in the same way.

Coordinating Conjunctions						
and	but	for	nor	or	so	yet

EXAMPLES On the end table were a reading lamp **and** some books.

Have you ever ridden a mule **or** a donkey?

The plane ran out of fuel, **but** the pilot glided it to a safe landing.

NOTE *For* is used as a conjunction when it connects independent clauses, usually in formal situations. Otherwise, *for* is a preposition.

(2) *Correlative conjunctions* are pairs of conjunctions that join words or groups of words used in the same way.

Correlative Conjunctions		
both . . . and	neither . . . nor	whether . . . or
either . . . or	not only . . . but also	

EXAMPLES Do you know **whether** Aunt Camilia **or** Uncle José will be there?

Your boots are **not only** wet **but also** muddy.

(3) A *subordinating conjunction* begins a subordinate clause, joining it to an independent clause.

Commonly Used Subordinating Conjunctions			
after	because	since	when
although	before	so that	whenever
as	even though	than	where
as if	how	that	wherever
as much as	if	though	whether
as soon as	in order that	unless	while
as though	provided that	until	why

EXAMPLES	Sit still **so that** the doctor can examine your bruise.
	Because it started raining, we had to rush for shelter.

1l An *interjection* is a word used to express emotion. It has no grammatical relation to other words in the sentence.

EXAMPLES	ah, ouch, hey, oh, well, whew, whoops, wow, yikes

EXERCISE 12   Identifying and Classifying Conjunctions

Underline the conjunctions in the following paragraph. In the space above each conjunction, write *COO* for *coordinating conjunction*, *COR* for *correlative conjunction*, or *SUB* for *subordinating conjunction*.

                                                                                COO
EX.   Snake charmers begin learning their craft at the age of five <u>or</u> six.

[1] Although the art of snake charming is less common today, it was an honored tradition in India and Egypt for thousands of years. [2] In India, snake charmers considered themselves to be a separate group, and they associated certain beliefs with their practices as well. [3] They viewed snake charming not only as an art, but also as a way of life. [4] When they were successful at it, they became part of a sacred tradition. [5] Since they had no other source of income, "snakers" staged the most dramatic performances possible. [6] Because the threat of danger attracts crowds, poisonous cobras were often used. [7] The snaker seemed to be charming the cobra with a flute, but having no ears, the snake couldn't actually hear anything. [8] The snake charmer attracted the snake and used various techniques to do so. [9] For example, the snake charmer might splash cold water on it or blow air on it through the flute. [10] While any of these methods could be used, the trick was always to keep the snake harmlessly "entranced" for the length of the show.

EXERCISE 13   Writing Sentences with Interjections

Write 10 sentences describing a heroic rescue. In your sentences, use at least four interjections from the list in section 11. Underline the interjections you use.

EX.   _Wow!_ _That bonfire is getting out of control!_

_____

_____

_____

_____

_____

_____

_____

_____

_____

_____

_____

_____

_____

_____

_____

_____

_____

_____

_____

_____

DETERMINING PARTS OF SPEECH

1m   A word's part of speech is determined by how the word is used in a sentence.

EXAMPLES   Have a **drink** of this freshly squeezed juice. [*Drink* is used as a noun.]

I **drink** orange juice every morning. [*Drink* is used as a verb.]

Colandra works **hard**. [*Hard* is used as an adverb to modify *works*.]

Misha fell onto the **hard** floor of the gym. [*Hard* is used as an adjective to modify *floor*.]

EXERCISE 14   Identifying Parts of Speech

Write the part of speech of each italicized word in the space above it. Write *N* for *noun*, *P* for *pronoun*, *V* for *verb*, *ADJ* for *adjective*, *ADV* for *adverb*, *PR* for *preposition*, *C* for *conjunction*, or *I* for *interjection*.

                      N   *V*

EX.   The case of *Johnny Red had* everyone baffled.

[1] It was a crying *shame* that *it* ever came to court. [2] Johnny Red, the *best* horse in the state, had failed to make his last *jump* in the *championship* competition. [3] Many people thought the *horse* trainer *had been* negligent. [4] This *fact* resulted in a *lawsuit* filed *by* Paula, who had been riding Johnny Red. [5] The courtroom was packed, *and* the judge *warned* people not to crowd the aisle. [6] Then the judge advised the seated jurors to listen *carefully to* all the testimony. [7] "Use your *brain* power," he told *them*. [8] "And don't talk to the *press* until the trial is *over*."

[9] The trainer had done little to win people's *trust* because of *his* strange ways. [10] For example, he was *occasionally* known to shoe his horses in *bright* colors. [11] At last, *his* friend Willimena got up on the *witness stand*.

[12] "*No!*" she exclaimed. "This man is a great trainer and couldn't be *responsible* for this." [13] Then, out of the *blue,* Paula, a witness, remembered seeing Red putting his *head over* the fence to munch on something the day of the competition.

[14] "As a matter of fact," added Paula, "I recall Red faltering *oddly* just before I started *to saddle* him up." [15] Luckily for the trainer, that *very* afternoon *detectives* were able to find out what Red *had eaten*.

MODULE 1: PARTS OF SPEECH
REVIEW EXERCISE 2

A.   Identifying Parts of Speech

Write the part of speech of each italicized word in the space above it. Write *N* for *noun*, *P* for *pronoun*, *V* for *verb*, *ADJ* for *adjective*, *ADV* for *adverb*, *PR* for *preposition*, *C* for *conjunction*, or *I* for *interjection*.

                    ADV   *ADJ*

EX.   Sequoyah will *forever* be remembered as one of the greatest *Native American* leaders.

[1] Born in Tennessee about 1770, Sequoyah *was raised* on a small farm by his *Cherokee* mother. [2] A childhood sickness made him lame *for* life, but it did not destroy *his* brave spirit. [3] *After* his mother died, he married a Cherokee woman named Sallie and went to Alabama to run a *trading post*. [4] As a result of his own *personal* struggle, he persuaded the *Cherokee Council* to pass prohibition laws. [5] Sequoyah's *family* was interested *in* preserving Cherokee traditions. [6] But Sequoyah wasn't interested *only* in the traditions of the *Cherokee* people. [7] He soon proved *himself* a talented artist, blacksmith, *and* silversmith. [8] *But* his *greatest* accomplishment was still to come. [9] *In* 1791, he saw some letters written by *white* soldiers. [10] He was fascinated *with* the idea *of* communicating by writing. [11] Sequoyah devoted his time to developing a similar form of *communication* for the *Cherokee people*. [12] Absorbed in *his* project, he spent *12* years inventing a system. [13] *Many* people *tried* to discourage him. [14] *Finally,* though, he created a symbol for each of the *85* sounds in the Cherokee language. [15] Self-educated, he *had invented* a new alphabet all *by* himself. [16] *Fortunately,* many others found *it* easy to learn. [17] Soon, *some* of the Cherokees used his *system* to write and publish books in their own language. [18] For his achievement, Sequoyah *has earned* a permanent place of *honor* in the history of his people. [19] Largely thanks to his work, the first issue *of* a *weekly* newspaper, <u>The Cherokee Phoenix</u>, was published in 1828. [20] In *recognition* of his great accomplishment, the giant redwoods of *California* were named for him, "Sequoyah gigantea."

MODULE 1: PARTS OF SPEECH
MODULE REVIEW

A.   Identifying Nouns, Pronouns, and Adjectives

Identify the part of speech of each italicized word or expression. On the line before each sentence, write *N* for *noun*, *P* for *pronoun*, or *ADJ* for *adjective*.

EX. ___*ADJ*___ *Bright* sunshine filled the room.

_____ 1. Diego wore blue jeans and a *cowboy* hat.

_____ 2. We swept the floor *ourselves*.

_____ 3. The little girl was *cranky* until she got some juice.

_____ 4. *Which* of these tangerines is ripe?

_____ 5. William loves *singing* in the car.

_____ 6. *Liberty* and justice for all are fine ideals.

_____ 7. My *cousin* Lyle lives in Massachusetts.

_____ 8. Pick *any* card you like, and I'll tell you what it is.

_____ 9. You take *this* crate, and I'll take that one.

_____ 10. To *whom* was he speaking?

B.   Determining the Parts of Speech of Words

In the paragraph below, identify the part of speech of each italicized word or expression. On the line before each sentence, write *N* for *noun*, *ADJ* for *adjective*, *P* for *pronoun*, *V* for *verb*, *ADV* for *adverb*, *PR* for *preposition*, *C* for *conjunction*, or *I* for *interjection*. Use a semicolon to separate your answers.

EX. ___*N;ADV*___ Driving on the *right* is a *fairly* new custom.

_____ 1. *Only* 200 years ago, *travelers* who met on the road would usually move to the left.

_____ 2. *This* is still the custom *in* England.

_____ 3. Pope Boniface VIII made left-hand travel the *official policy* in Europe in 1300 CE.

_____ 4. *This* rule applied to all the people coming *to* Rome.

_____ 5. Researchers say the custom makes sense *because* most people *are* right-handed.

_____ 6. Left-handed travel makes it easier for a person to respond *if* trouble occurs.

_____ 7. In countries influenced by Great Britain, *left-handed* travel is still customary.

_____ 8. However, that practice is not carried out in the *United States*.

_____ 9. Believe it *or* not, the reason has to do with wagons.

_____ 10. Most North American settlers' wagons *had* no front seats, so the driver sat instead on the left-rear animal in the team.

_____ 11. Drivers sat to the left so they could *better* control their teams of horses or oxen with their right hands.

_____ 12. In this situation, drivers could also keep an eye *on* each other's wagon wheels passing to their left.

_____ 13. In this way, they more easily *avoided* accidents. *Phew!*

_____ 14. British wagons, meanwhile, had seats, and *their* drivers sat on the right.

_____ 15. Consequently, in modern *British* cars, the steering wheels are also positioned on the right.

C. Writing Sentences with Words Used as Specific Parts of Speech

Write sentences according to the guidelines below.

EX. Use *building* as a verb.
The children are building a sandcastle.

1. Use *both* as an adjective. _____

2. Use *well* as a noun. _____

3. Use *whew* as an interjection. _____

4. Use *turn* as a linking verb. _____

5. Use *unless* as a subordinating conjunction. _____

_____

6. Use *next to* as a preposition. _____

7. Use *outside* as an adverb. _____

8. Use *who* as a relative pronoun. _____

9. Use *not only, but also* as a correlative conjunction. _____

_____

10. Use *turn* as an action verb. _____

SUBJECTS AND PREDICATES

2a   A sentence consists of two parts: the *subject* and the *predicate*. The subject tells *whom* or *what* the sentence is about. The predicate tells something about the subject.

	SUBJECT	PREDICATE		PREDICATE	SUBJECT
EXAMPLES	Water |	spilled.		Away on the ship sailed |	the crew.

	SUBJECT	PREDICATE		PREDICATE	SUBJECT	PREDICATE
	Dina |	brought the salad.		When will |	you and Sal |	arrive?

2b   The *simple subject* is the main word or group of words that tells *whom* or *what* the sentence is about.

EXAMPLES   **Who** was the performer in that concert?
Walking to the bus stop, **Antonio** whistled his favorite song.

2c   The *simple predicate* is a verb or verb phrase that tells something about the subject.

EXAMPLES   Pauline **was** restless and bored.
Did Omar **memorize** his lines for the show?

NOTE   In this module, the term *subject* refers to the simple subject, and the term *verb* refers to the simple predicate (a one-word verb or a verb phrase) unless otherwise indicated.

EXERCISE 1   Identifying Complete Subjects and Predicates in Sentences

In each sentence, draw a vertical line or lines to separate the complete subject from the predicate.

EX.   Waiting for the bus to arrive, Sasha \| read two chapters in her mystery book.

1. Who was your favorite actor in that movie?
2. Jorge arranged the grapes, apples, and oranges in a ceramic bowl.
3. George threw back the covers of his bed.
4. Magda noticed the blooming cherry trees in the park.
5. Which herbal tea is the healthiest?
6. Instead of going to the concert, Francesca studied for her Spanish exam.
7. The tree boughs drooped under the weight of the wet snow.

8. Into the bushes fled the frightened rabbit.

9. To stay strong, I practice yoga every other day.

10. A group of college students protested the city's street repair plan.

11. Yori recognized the constellation to the south.

12. Meeting at the library, many volunteers prepared for the book sale.

13. The dress rehearsal for *Fiddler on the Roof* will be after school tomorrow.

14. Is the cat sleeping on the windowsill?

15. Lessons in breathing, floating, and kicking were taught to the young swimmers.

16. Feeding on sunflower seeds every day, one gray squirrel grew chubbier than the others.

17. The tired physician leaned back in her chair for a short nap.

18. Blueberry bagels are a popular breakfast item in our household.

19. Having read *The Hunger Games*, everyone enjoyed seeing the film adaptation.

20. Did Anton visit his grandparents in St. Petersburg?

EXERCISE 2   Identifying Subjects and Verbs in Sentences

In each sentence below, underline the subject once and the verb twice.

EX.   The <u>skier</u> <u>maneuvered</u> expertly through the course.

1. Where did your sister go to college?

2. All of the packages were delivered.

3. Sunning itself on the porch, the dog stretched lazily.

4. Several awards were presented by Congress today.

5. Gregg will play point guard this season.

6. Did Elena ever find her chemistry assignment?

7. Encouraged by her lead, Laura ran swiftly to the finish line.

8. Apples spilled from the basket onto the table.

9. Into the bright sea sailed the tall ship.

10. When will your family return from vacation?

2d   A *compound subject* consists of two or more subjects that are joined by a conjunction and have the same verb.

Compound subjects are usually joined by *and* or *or*.

COMPOUND SUBJECT   VERB

EXAMPLES   The <u>cat</u> and her <u>kittens</u> | <u><u>slept</u></u> in the hall closet last night.

COMPOUND SUBJECT   VERB

<u>Sam, Marlon</u>, and <u>Pedro</u> | <u><u>rode</u></u> their horses through the woods.

2e   A *compound verb* consists of two or more verbs that are joined by a conjunction and have the same subject.

Compound verbs are usually joined by *and*, *but*, or *or*.

SUBJECT   COMPOUND VERB

EXAMPLES   <u>Lisette</u> | <u><u>walks</u></u> or <u><u>jogs</u></u> along the rail trail.

SUBJECT   COMPOUND VERB

For the dinner party, <u>I</u> | <u><u>prepared</u></u> pasta and <u><u>baked</u></u> bread.

EXERCISE 3   Identifying Compound Subjects and Compound Verbs

In the sentences below, underline the subjects once and the verbs twice.

EX.   <u>Katia</u> and <u>Suzanne</u> <u><u>write</u></u> and <u><u>publish</u></u> short stories.

1. Water lapped against the sand and tickled our toes.
2. The coach and her team won the game and celebrated their victory.
3. Snow and ice threatened their holiday travel plans.
4. Anticipation and excitement kept Manuel awake most of the night.
5. Each of the children studied and excelled in a different language.
6. Kazuo and Taro flew to Japan and visited their father's family.
7. At home, Tamara and Misha speak in Russian and English.
8. The plane and its passengers had been delayed.
9. Having adapted to arid conditions, many plants and animals live and thrive in the desert.
10. At Sam's party, we ate a lot, played music, and danced.

EXERCISE 4 Using Compound Subjects and Compound Verbs to Combine Sentences

Combine each group of short sentences into one longer sentence by using compound subjects and compound verbs. Write each new sentence on the lines provided. Underline the subject once and the verb twice.

EX. The captain alerted his crew to the approaching storm. He ordered everyone to wear life jackets.

The <u>captain</u> <u><u>alerted</u></u> his crew to the approaching storm and <u><u>ordered</u></u> everyone to wear life jackets.

1. Before going outside, Rena put on a coat. Rinda put on a coat, too.

2. The guests arrived on Thursday night. They didn't leave until Monday.

3. Marta is learning how to play Go. Jamal and Mark are learning, too.

4. After cleaning the attic, Franklin sorted old photographs. Then he called his sister. Franklin invited his sister to dinner.

5. When steamed and served with fresh lemon, broccoli tastes crisp and zesty. Green beans are crisp and zesty when served this way, too.

6. Last week, Bruce played in the open jazz competition. He played the saxophone. Roberto played the saxophone, too.

7. After the dress rehearsal, Miriam walked home. Then she ate dinner. Finally, she practiced her lines one more time.

8. The young couple replastered the old ceilings. Then they sanded the plaster. Finally, they painted the ceilings.

9. Amanda took the reins from Kevin. She mounted the horse.

10. *David Copperfield* is a great novel by Charles Dickens. *Bleak House* and *Great Expectations* are also great novels by Dickens.

MODULE 2: THE SENTENCE

FINDING THE SUBJECT OF A SENTENCE

2f   To find the subject of a sentence, ask *Who?* or *What?* before the verb.

EXAMPLES   Blocking my view of the harbor was a building. [*What* was blocking my view? A *building* was.]

In her office, Ms. Menino graded papers. [*Who* graded papers? *Ms. Menino* graded them.]

(1)   The subject of a sentence expressing a command or a request is always understood to be *you*, although *you* may not appear in the sentence.

EXAMPLES   Watch that movie to learn more about oceans. [*Who* is being told to watch? *You* are being told to watch.]

Please listen to my speech, Ann. [*Who* is being asked to listen? *You* listen.]

(2)   The subject of a sentence is never in a prepositional phrase.

EXAMPLES   A **group** of students gathered around the bulletin board. [*Who* gathered? A *group* gathered. *Students* is the object of the preposition *of.*]

One of the restaurants on that street has closed down. [*What* has closed down? *One* has closed down. *Restaurants* is the object of the preposition *of. Street* is the object of the preposition *on.*]

(3)   The subject of a sentence expressing a question usually follows the verb or a part of the verb phrase.

EXAMPLES   Is **Rudy** moving next week? [*Who* is moving next week? *Rudy* is.]

Will the **festival** end on Sunday? [*What* will end on Sunday? The *festival* will end.]

EXERCISE 5   Finding Subjects and Verbs

In each sentence, underline the subject once and the verb twice. Include all parts of a compound subject or a compound verb and all words in a verb phrase. In sentences that give orders or make requests, underline only the verb.

EX.   That night, both <u>websites</u> and television <u>stations</u> <u>aired</u> the president's address in its entirety.

1. Throughout her lifetime, the philanthropist collected and donated works of art.

2. Swooping over the lake were seagulls and ducks.

3. A herd of elephants bathed and played in the muddy river.

4. Turn left, and follow the signs at the next intersection.

5. The printmaker and his assistant experimented with different inks.

6. After the exam, Marla, Theresa, and Jamie met in the hallway and walked home together.

7. Lush ferns and May apples carpeted the floor of the pine grove.

8. After her evening jog, Janet made a salad.

9. Gregory and Margaret registered for their first judo class.

10. Sunflower seeds and millet are healthy bread ingredients.

11. After his illness, the musician practiced and started performing again.

12. Each night, the cat paced the hallways and looked for mice.

13. The host always opened and closed her show with the same song.

14. Mr. Martínez and Ms. Chung have earned good citizenship awards and were honored by the mayor.

15. The diner and the bookstore on the corner have closed.

16. Crumpled paper covered the surface of the drafting table.

17. Whales and icebergs are common sights off the coast of Alaska.

18. Hiding behind the tree were Alice and Anton.

19. City hall has been remodeled and opens tomorrow.

20. In her backyard, Felicia stood and watched the lunar eclipse.

21. The student's excellent academic record and community service earned her a scholarship.

22. Each fall, the northern peninsula of Wisconsin shimmers with changing leaves and hosts thousands of visitors.

23. A group of citizens attended the meeting and voiced their opinions.

24. Peonies in pink, magenta, and crimson grow in that garden.

25. In Mr. Rasko's basement, birdhouses and feeders were being built and painted.

DIRECT OBJECTS AND INDIRECT OBJECTS

2g A *complement* is a word or a group of words that completes the meaning of a verb.

Some sentences contain only a subject and a verb.

              S V

EXAMPLES   She ran.

              V

           Look! [The subject *you* is understood.]

Other sentences require one or more complements to complete their meaning.

INCOMPLETE   Melvin bought

  COMPLETE   Melvin bought a **hamster**.

Most sentences include at least one complement.

The ***direct object*** and the ***indirect object*** are two types of complements.

2h A *direct object* is a noun or a pronoun that receives the action of a verb or shows the result of the action. A direct object tells *whom* or *what* the action of a transitive verb involves.

EXAMPLES   Rachel admired **Jane Goodall**. [Admired *whom*? *Jane Goodall*.]
              That man delivered **flowers** to my house. [Delivered *what*? *Flowers*.]

NOTE   For emphasis, the direct object may come before the subject and the verb.

        EXAMPLE   What an exciting **movie** we watched! [Watched *what*? A *movie*.]

2i An *indirect object* is a noun or a pronoun that comes between a transitive verb and its direct object. It tells *to whom* or *to what* or *for whom* or *for what* the action of the verb is done.

EXAMPLES   Diego read **Ms. Hintz** and **Mr. Saenz** his poetry. [Read *to whom*? *Ms. Hintz* and *Mr. Saenz*.]
              I gave the **house** a cleaning. [Gave *to what*? The *house*.]

Don't mistake an object of the preposition *to* or *for* for an indirect object.

    INDIRECT OBJECT   The teacher gave **Todd** and **me** a makeup test.
OBJECT OF PREPOSITION   The teacher gave a makeup test to **Todd** and **me**.

EXERCISE 6   Identifying Direct and Indirect Objects

Underline the direct and indirect objects in the following sentences. In the space above the underlined words, write *DO* for *direct object* or *IO* for *indirect object*. Some sentences have more than one object, and not all sentences contain an indirect object.

                      IO   *DO*

EX.   Derek showed the <u>volunteer</u> his voter registration <u>card</u>.

1. Nana gave her granddaughter the ruby ring.

2. The journalist interviewed the scientists before they entered the laboratory.

3. After the snowfall, Uncle Vanya sculpted my cousins and me a statue out of ice

    and snow.

4. Mrs. Mantuano feeds the cardinals small, black sunflower seeds.

5. Sylvana's strong language skills have earned her a scholarship.

6. For dinner, my father made us barley soup, salad, and Challah.

7. We rode the elevator to the top floor of the John Hancock building.

8. After much persuasion, Mom finally showed us photos of her as a child.

9. Franz Schubert composed sonatas, quartets, and symphonies.

10. Erica donates her time and skills to the area literacy center.

11. What a stunning exhibit about Egypt we saw!

12. Before leaving, Helen gave Frank instructions about collecting the mail.

13. Tomás covers sporting events for the West High *Herald*.

14. Jasper gave Bill the term paper and asked for his opinion.

15. Stanley offered us excellent seats in the theater.

16. Jacob declined the apples and took the pitcher of cider.

17. Flooding destroyed many houses and farms.

18. Cam handed his father a birthday card.

19. Ice covered the roads and kept us from traveling.

20. We welcomed the Chans' invitation to the party.

21. The scientist showed us aerial photographs of glaciers on Mount Everest.

22. The sales associate sold the customer two pairs of pants and a sweater.

23. Warm weather brightened our spirits.

24. What a marvelous performance the cover band gave us!

25. Sheila practiced the long list of vocabulary words for her French exam.

OBJECTIVE COMPLEMENTS

2j   An *objective complement* is a word or group of words that helps complete the
meaning of an action verb by identifying or modifying the direct object.

EXAMPLES   Kyle called Rita a brilliant **mathematician**.
            Jerome painted the model airplane **gray**.

Only a few verbs take an objective complement: *consider*, *make*, and verbs that can be
replaced by *consider* or *make*, such as *appoint*, *call*, *choose*, *elect*, *name*, *paint*, and *sweep*.

EXERCISE 7   Identifying Objective Complements

Underline each objective complement in the sentences below.

EX.   Programmers considered the new app <u>brilliant</u>.

1. Stefan painted the front porch steps green.

2. Many found the Supreme Court's decision amazing.

3. Advertisements called the new car sleek and sophisticated.

4. Always forgetful, John considered his brother a fountain of knowledge.

5. The sleet and snow made the rural routes treacherous.

6. Taylor called Jiro a true and trusted friend.

7. The school board appointed Ms. Guerra interim president.

8. Elena and Bob named their daughter Lara.

9. An art expert called the painting a fake, but others disagreed.

10. Friends nominated Jerry cochair of the food collection drive.

11. Frank named his two gerbils Romeo and Juliet.

12. Every Saturday morning, the shop owner wipes the windows clean.

13. Deeply concerned, the doctor thought the patient's condition serious.

14. Officials found the heavy voter turnout a surprise.

15. Even my friend Marsha called the story sad.

REVIEW EXERCISE

A. Finding Subjects and Verbs

In the sentences below, underline the subject(s) once and the verb(s) twice. Include all parts of a compound subject or a compound verb.

> EX.   On Saturday mornings, <u>Shaniqua</u> and <u>Ivan</u> <u>walk</u> to the community center.

1. At the center, they meet their reading partners, Joel and Yolanda.
2. Joel and Shaniqua are reading short stories and poems by Raymond Carver.
3. Stories and plays by Anton Chekhov are familiar to Ivan, but not to Yolanda.
4. Yolanda has read some of Chekhov's descriptions and likes them.
5. Ivan agrees, but he does not enjoy some of the sadder stories.

B. Identifying Direct Objects, Indirect Objects, and Objective Complements

On the line before each sentence, identify the italicized complement by writing *DO* for *direct object*, *IO* for *indirect object*, or *OC* for *objective complement*.

> EX. ___*OC*___   We consider the tomato a *fruit*.

_____ 1. Between the pages, the old dictionary contained numerous pressed *flowers*.

_____ 2. Lettuce picked from the garden makes a salad *fresh* and tasty.

_____ 3. Dogs have tremendous *abilities* as thoughtful, inquisitive, and loyal companions.

_____ 4. The environmentalists gave our *company* advice on irrigation.

_____ 5. Carla thought the mountain path treacherous and *beautiful*.

_____ 6. Some of the ancient Egyptian jars contained *honey*.

_____ 7. Shannon's portrait of her grandfather won the grand *prize* at the Missouri State Fair.

_____ 8. The diners gave the *chef* several compliments on the fine meal.

_____ 9. We painted the old car *green*.

_____ 10. After much debate, the panel finally called the matter *closed*.

SUBJECT COMPLEMENTS

2k A *predicate nominative* is a word or group of words that follows a linking verb and refers to the same person or thing as the subject of the verb.

EXAMPLES Dr. Chan is a **pediatrician**. [The noun *pediatrician* refers to the subject, *Dr. Chan.*]

The three contestants are **Juliana**, **Lucian**, and **Marco**. [The compound *Juliana, Lucian, and Marco* refers to the subject, *contestants.*]

2l A *predicate adjective* is an adjective that follows a linking verb and modifies the subject of the verb.

EXAMPLES Iona looks **relaxed**. [The adjective *relaxed* modifies the subject, *Iona.*]

My new puppy is **active**. [The adjective *active* modifies the subject, *puppy.*]

EXERCISE 8 Identifying Linking Verbs and Subject Complements

In each sentence, underline the subject complement once and the linking verb twice. On the line before the sentence, identify the complement by writing *PN* for *predicate nominative* or *PA* for *predicate adjective.*

EX. *PA* Does that apple taste tart?

_____ 1. Of these three fabrics, the velvet is the one I'll buy.

_____ 2. Our state's chief industries are agriculture and tourism.

_____ 3. After the storm subsided, the lake became calm.

_____ 4. Grapefruit can taste bitter or sour.

_____ 5. The tall stalk with broad green leaves is a Brussels sprouts plant.

_____ 6. All of the contestants looked nervous.

_____ 7. Ava's drawings are sensitive and powerful.

_____ 8. After her walk, Mrs. Petrakis felt energetic and refreshed.

_____ 9. Peanut butter is a good protein source for vegetarians.

_____ 10. Before the announcement, the mood in the room was electric.

_____ 11. The two candidates for class president are Julia and Eli.

_____ 12. Wearing a cape and dark glasses, the man looked mysterious.

_____ 13. The pine cones and evergreen boughs felt sticky from the sap.

_____ 14. Of the two fragrances, this one smells sweeter.

_____ 15. The tree with the crimson leaves is a red maple.

_____ 16. After the reading, the young author looked relieved.

_____ 17. During the flood, the citizens remained hopeful of saving their homes.

_____ 18. Many species of eucalyptus trees are aromatic.

_____ 19. We learned that our neighbor is an accomplished pianist.

_____ 20. Toward the end of the long lecture, the professor's voice sounded raspy and dry.

EXERCISE 9   Writing Complements

Complete each sentence below with the type of subject complement named in parentheses. Write your answers on the lines provided.

EX.   The tall pines in the forest are __lovely__. (*predicate adjective*)

1. During a summer storm, the sound of rain on the roof is _____. (*predicate adjective*)

2. Our great-aunt Isabel was _____. (*predicate nominative*)

3. Waiting in the lobby, the applicants for the position looked _____ and _____. (*compound predicate adjective*)

4. The owner of the small bungalow on our block is _____. (*predicate nominative*)

5. My two favorite performers are _____ and _____. (*compound predicate nominative*)

6. Especially without their leaves, the trees look _____ and _____. (*compound predicate adjective*)

7. Why does the vegetable soup taste _____? (*predicate adjective*)

8. Two popular apples are _____ and _____. (*compound predicate nominative*)

9. The chorus sounded _____. (*predicate adjective*)

10. After the announcement, the winner looked _____ and _____. (*compound predicate adjective*)

A. Identifying Subjects and Verbs in a Paragraph

In the paragraph below, underline the subjects once and the verbs twice.

EX. Surprisingly, bagpipes originated in Asia.

[1] Some people find bagpipes a shrill instrument, but others fall in love with them. [2] Actually, bagpipes are two instruments in one. [3] Blowing into the instrument, the player fills the bag with air. [4] Then the player squeezes the bag with their arm and forces air through two kinds of pipes. [5] Three drones and a chanter are the pipes for a modern bagpipe. [6] Air goes into the drones to create predetermined notes. [7] After starting a song, the player cannot tune the drones. [8] The rest of the air goes to the chanter. [9] The chanter has seven finger stops and a thumb stop.

[10] To produce different notes, the musician places fingers on the stops in the chanter.

B. Identifying Complements in Sentences

Underline the complement or complements in each sentence. On the line before the sentence, classify each complement by writing *DO* for *direct object*, *IO* for *indirect object*, *OC* for *objective complement*, *PN* for *predicate nominative*, or *PA* for *predicate adjective*.

EX. *PN* As a young woman, our grandmother was a seamstress.

_____ 1. Famous for his sophistication and wry humor, George Clooney made many films.

_____ 2. After kneading the dough, Dad formed two round loaves.

_____ 3. The guitarist was a master of Spanish flamenco music.

_____ 4. Even the most experienced art critics considered her photographs wonderful.

_____ 5. Before putting out the campfire, Ben poured Sam a mug of hot cider.

_____ 6. After calling, please confirm your order by email.

_____ 7. The blue satin dress looked elegant and refined.

_____ 8. The seemingly quiet, well-mannered cat was an accomplished hunter.

_____ 9. In a strong, clear voice, she read her poems to the hushed audience.

10. Some analysts predict high inflation before an economic recession.

11. The new play at the Center for Performing Arts is a guaranteed success.

12. After a vigorous swim, Alisha usually feels refreshed.

13. To avoid fines, please return your library books on time.

14. What an outstanding athlete she is!

15. Halim missed the concert by hours.

C. Writing a News Article

You are a writer for a local news website. Your job is to take notes over the telephone from a reporter and write a first draft of a news article. Use the notes below to write an article of at least 10 sentences. You will need to create other details to finish the article. Underline and label at least one compound verb, one compound subject, one direct object, and one indirect object in your article. Don't forget to give your article a headline.

Who?	Roberto and Sarah Serran
What?	an alligator crashing through a screen door to get into the house
When?	August 3, 2023; 3:45 p.m.
Why?	seemed to be after the people's pet poodle
Where?	Neiberville, Florida
How?	used its strength to ram the screen, tearing a hole in it

EX.   *A Strange Guest*

COMPOUND SUBJECT

Yesterday afternoon, a Florida <u>couple</u> and their pet <u>poodle</u> were relaxing in their living room.

_____

_____

_____

_____

_____

_____

_____

_____

_____

MODULE 3: THE PHRASE

PREPOSITIONAL PHRASES

3a A *phrase* is a group of words that is used as a single part of speech and does not contain a verb and its subject.

3b A *prepositional phrase* is a group of words consisting of a preposition, a noun or pronoun that serves as the object of the preposition, and any modifiers of that object.

EXAMPLES The tiny room **off the kitchen** is Maria's study. [The noun *kitchen* is the object of the preposition *off*.]

The lawsuit finally went **to the grand jury**. [The compound noun *grand jury* is the object of the preposition *to*.]

According to her, a larger room would never feel cozy. [The pronoun *her* is the object of the preposition *According to*.]

The object of a preposition may be compound.

EXAMPLE She has covered the walls **with posters and photographs**.

EXERCISE 1   Identifying Prepositional Phrases and Their Objects

Find the prepositional phrases in the following sentences. Underline each preposition once and the object of the preposition twice.

EX.   My baseball cards are <u>in</u> the <u>closet</u>.

1. Please take the package to the post office.
2. There's not enough room on my desk for this project.
3. Could we go to the football game, Mom?
4. I lost my pen through a hole in my backpack.
5. These boots are quite warm because they are lined with wool.
6. Does hanging a horseshoe above a door bring good luck?
7. I don't have a mean bone in my body.
8. Tala scrubbed the ink on the wall with a sponge.
9. If a tree falls in the forest, only the birds will hear it.
10. Put it there, near the microwave.
11. They heard a grating noise after each shifting of the gears.
12. I walked around the block first.
13. If you moved from here, where would you go?
14. No, don't go that way; go over the bridge and turn right.
15. Shelly lined the first pitch into short right field.

EXERCISE 2   Revising Sentences Using Prepositional Phrases

In each sentence below, add at least one prepositional phrase as a modifier.

    EX.   Botan forgot his jacket.   *Botan forgot his jacket at school.*

1. Don't be alarmed.

   _____

2. We are invited.

   _____

3. Have you ever gone swimming?

   _____

4. My brother has a blister.

   _____

5. I took this picture.

   _____

6. We brought our own shovels.

   _____

7. If Jody doesn't return the books, who will?

   _____

8. I like to wear a sweater.

   _____

9. We went and nearly got lost.

   _____

10. The Drapers had a great time.

    _____

11. Did you see the Weeknd when he performed?

    _____

12. I packed a cheese sandwich.

    _____

13. The dog took a long nap.

    _____

14. My friends arrived.

    _____

15. A vegetable pizza is baking.

    _____

ADJECTIVE PHRASES AND ADVERB PHRASES

3c An *adjective phrase* is a prepositional phrase that modifies a noun or a pronoun.

An adjective phrase tells *what kind*, *how many*, or *which one*.

EXAMPLES   Two cups **of peppermint tea** is my limit. [*Of peppermint tea* modifies the noun *cups*.]

Everyone **in the classroom** was absolutely silent. [*In the classroom* modifies the pronoun *Everyone*.]

3d An *adverb phrase* is a prepositional phrase that modifies a verb, an adjective, or an adverb.

An adverb phrase tells *how, when, where, why*, or *to what extent* (*how long* or *how far*).

EXAMPLES   New Zealand was first inhabited **by the Maori**. [*By the Maori* modifies the verb *was inhabited*.]

The Maori canoes were full **of people, animals, plants, and tools**. [*Of people, animals, plants, and tools* modifies the adjective *full*.]

Why did the Maori travel so far **from their home**? [*From their home* modifies the adverb *far*.]

EXERCISE 3   Identifying Adjective Phrases and Adverb Phrases and the Words They Modify

Underline each adjective phrase once and each adverb phrase twice. Draw an arrow from the phrase to the word(s) it modifies.

EX.   Dad and I went to the grocery store on the corner.

1. We bought food for our two-night backpacking trip.

2. Dad took a day's vacation from work.

3. We had been planning the trip since last month.

4. At home we prepared the food.

5. Everything except the water went into little plastic bags.

6. We loaded our backpacks with socks, sweaters, and the food.

7. Finally, we tied our sleeping bags to the bottoms of our backpacks.

8. After a long hike, we reached our campsite.

9. The next morning, we awoke before sunrise.

10. We loaded the sleeping bags and backpacks into the car again.

11. It was still dark as we drove along the empty freeway.

12. At last we arrived at the trailhead parking lot.

13. We put our boots on and walked beside each other for a while.

14. We rested once or twice along the way.

15. Dad sat down next to me, and we looked at the morning sky together.

EXERCISE 4   Writing Instructions

You and your family plan to take a trip to the beach, but you want to make sure no one forgets anything they may need for the day. Write a set of instructions on what to pack, including food, sunscreen, and other necessities. Include at least five adjective phrases and five adverb phrases. Underline each adjective phrase once and each adverb phrase twice.

_____

_____

_____

_____

_____

_____

_____

_____

_____

_____

_____

_____

_____

_____

_____

3e A *participle* **is a verb form that can be used as an adjective.**

Two kinds of participles are the *present participle* and the *past participle*. The perfect tense of a participle is formed with a past participle and the helping verb *having*.

PRESENT **Waving**, the boy dwindled to a speck as the boat went west. [*Waving*, a form of the verb *wave*, modifies the noun *boy*.]

Did you see anyone **walking** through the backyard? [*Walking*, a form of the verb *walk*, modifies the pronoun *anyone*.]

PAST Di and Wendy tossed the **baked** potato back and forth to cool it. [*Baked*, a form of the verb *bake*, modifies the noun *potato*.]

Battered and **soaked**, we held on to the overturned skiff. [*Battered*, a form of the verb *batter*, and *soaked*, a form of the verb *soak*, modify the pronoun *we*.]

PERFECT The dancer, **having spent** countless hours practicing, performed the routine perfectly. [*Having spent*, a form of the verb *spend*, modifies the noun *dancer*.]

Having napped, the four-year-old was ready to play. [*Having napped*, a form of the verb *nap*, modifies the compound noun *four-year-old*.]

3f A *participial phrase* **consists of a participle and all of the words related to the participle.**

EXAMPLES **Talking to her dog**, Mildred repotted the four azaleas. [The phrase modifies the noun *Mildred*.]

The outfielder, **having scooped up the grounder**, threw the ball to first base. [The phrase modifies the noun *outfielder*.]

Paco, **having already learned the secret**, laughed at our impatient curiosity. [The phrase modifies the noun *Paco*.]

EXERCISE 5   Identifying Participles

Underline the participles used as adjectives in the following sentences.

EX.   Are those antique <u>cooking</u> utensils?

1. The shingled house barely survived the storm.
2. My grandpa likes stewed tomatoes.

3. In the fading light, Bly liked to watch the shorebirds gather.

4. Having showered, Dan was dismayed to find there were no clean towels.

5. I understand the northern spotted owl is an endangered species.

6. Lucy wanted a new fishing pole to replace the broken one.

7. All main dishes come with salad and a baked potato.

8. How much spending money do you have each week?

9. Do you suppose Kyle Larson's family buys him driving gloves for his birthday?

10. He carefully placed the polished guitar in its case.

11. Arnie ran away from the honking geese.

12. A draft blew the wrinkled curtains away from the window.

13. Toshi, having walked to school, had snow on her hair and shoulders.

14. Bagged newspapers are easy for the recycling crew to handle.

15. Running children and crying babies seemed to fill the tiny room.

EXERCISE 6   Identifying Participial Phrases and the Words They Modify

In each sentence below, underline the participial phrase once. Then underline twice the word(s) each participial phrase modifies.

EX. <u>Having grown up in a poor family</u>, <u>Pancho Gonzales</u> was not a member of a tennis club.

1. The name given to him at birth was Richard Alonzo Gonzales.

2. Born in Los Angeles in 1928, Pancho became the best U.S. tennis player of his day.

3. Living in Southern California, he could play tennis year-round.

4. Pancho, competing at a high level without a coach, had amazing success.

5. His playing, known for its speed and fierce attack, was always exciting.

6. Having turned professional in 1949, Pancho held several amateur titles.

7. Completing his final year as an amateur, he won six major tournaments.

8. As a professional, he dominated the U.S. men's singles circuit, winning the championship seven years in a row.

9. Whether playing on clay or on grass courts, he would win.

10. Admired for his powerful serves, Pancho always had a great number of enthusiastic fans.

GERUNDS AND GERUND PHRASES

3g   A *gerund* is a verb form ending in *-ing* that is used as a noun.

SUBJECT	**Skipping** rope is good exercise.
PREDICATE NOMINATIVE	A popular activity at Leo's house is **singing**.
DIRECT OBJECT	For two hours the forwards practiced **dribbling**.
INDIRECT OBJECT	Why not give **bricklaying** a try?
OBJECT OF A PREPOSITION	I talked to Amanda about **bowling**.

Don't confuse a gerund with a present participle used as an adjective or as part of a verb phrase.

GERUND	My favorite hobby is **working** on my car. [*Working* is a predicate nominative referring to the noun *hobby*.]
PRESENT PARTICIPLES	The crew was no longer **working**. [*Working* is the main verb in the verb phrase *was working*.]
	Working for this company, you will get excellent benefits. [*Working* is adjective modifying the pronoun *you*.]

NOTE   When a noun or pronoun comes before a gerund, the possessive form is usually used. However, when the noun or pronoun follows a preposition, the possessive is optional.

EXAMPLES   **Rachel's** reading was getting better.
I enjoy listening to **Rachel** [or **Rachel's**] reading.

3h   A *gerund phrase* consists of a gerund and all of the words related to the gerund.

Like participles, gerunds may have modifiers and complements.

EXAMPLES   **Having two national languages** can be an asset. [The phrase is the subject of the verb *can be*.]

My immediate goal is **running in the marathon**. [The phrase is a predicate nominative explaining the noun *goal*.]

My brother tried **singing the blues**. [The phrase is the direct object of the verb *tried*.]

Everyone applauded Harry and Bill for **boxing fairly**. [The phrase is the object of the preposition *for*.]

EXERCISE 7   Identifying Gerunds and Their Uses

Underline the gerunds in the sentences below. On the line before each sentence, identify how each gerund is used. Write *S* for *subject*, *PN* for *predicate nominative*, *DO* for *direct object*, or *OP* for *object of a preposition*.

EX. __*S*__   Travis's <u>singing</u> is terrific.

_____ 1. Jogging is great, but you shouldn't overdo it.

_____ 2. I took the train home in December because I don't enjoy flying.

_____ 3. My cousin Alma gave a speech about marketing last Tuesday afternoon.

_____ 4. I know that studying for this class is important.

_____ 5. On the baseball field, we practiced sliding.

_____ 6. Jamari's favorite art form is sculpting.

_____ 7. Tracing is a good way to create a design.

_____ 8. My kitten's purring can be heard across the room.

_____ 9. Ralph knows a lot about cooking.

_____ 10. One helpful and important skill is reading.

EXERCISE 8   Identifying Gerund Phrases and Their Uses

Underline the gerund phrases in the paragraph below. Above each gerund phrase, identify its use by writing *S* for *subject*, *PN* for *predicate nominative*, *DO* for *direct object*, or *OP* for *object of a preposition*.

EX.   <u>Going to the library</u> is a fun alternative to internet research.
        S

[1] I started my research by going to the town library. [2] My favorite pastime there is browsing in the stacks of books. [3] Going to the reference room took me by the science fiction shelves, where a book caught my eye. [4] I suppose whoever arranged the library enjoys trapping unwary researchers that way. [5] The next thing I knew, the librarian was talking about closing the library.

INFINITIVES AND INFINITIVE PHRASES

3i   An *infinitive* is a verb form that can be used as a noun, an adjective, or an adverb. An infinitive usually begins with *to.*

NOUN	Parents are excited once their baby learns **to smile.**
ADJECTIVE	The loan officer is the one **to ask.**
ADVERB	Molly came **to help.**

The word *to*, the sign of the infinitive, is sometimes omitted.

EXAMPLES   Let's **[to] visit** the Neimans.

Would you help Nalani **[to] stand** on her head?

The paint fumes made me **[to] faint.**

3j   An *infinitive phrase* consists of an infinitive and all the words related to the infinitive.

EXAMPLES   Do you try **to eat a balanced diet**? [The phrase is the direct object of the verb *Do try.*]

To read the morning paper in her robe and slippers seems indulgent to Rosa. [The phrase is the subject of the verb *seems.*]

Richard made a promise **to go to Tula Springs**. [The phrase modifies the noun *promise.*]

With a high-pressure hose, Joann was able **to scrape the paint in one day**. [The phrase modifies the predicate adjective *able.*]

NOTE   Unlike other verbals, an infinitive may have a subject. Such a construction is called an *infinitive clause*. The subject of an infinitive is in the objective case.

EXAMPLES   We thought **Paola to be the best choice**. [*Paola* is the subject of the infinitive *to be.* The entire clause is the direct object of the verb *thought.*]

Mr. Suro expected **him to come back for his change**. [*Him* is the subject of the infinitive *to come.* The entire clause is the direct object of the verb *expected.*]

EXERCISE 9   Identifying Infinitives

Underline the infinitives in the following paragraph.

EX.   Lani wanted <u>to run</u> for the student senate.

[1] While running, she began to learn more about democracy. [2] She decided to read a book about different governments. [3] In some ways, the students were able to govern themselves democratically. [4] The students voted to choose the best candidate for the senate. [5] Like the U.S. Congress, the elected students met to talk about issues and to vote on rule changes. [6] If people want to dismiss their representative, a democracy allows impeachment. [7] However, the students in Lani's class had never tried to dismiss their senator. [8] To impeach a student senator had not been necessary in the school. [9] Lani and her supporters wanted to add this ability to the school rules. [10] After Lani was elected, she was able to propose this rule change to the senate.

EXERCISE 10   Identifying Infinitive Phrases and Their Functions

Underline the infinitive phrases in the sentences below. On the line before each sentence, identify the way the phrase is used by writing *N* for *noun*, *ADJ* for *adjective*, or *ADV* for *adverb*. If the infinitive phrase is used as a noun, identify its function by writing *S* for *subject*, *DO* for *direct object*, or *PN* for *predicate nominative*. If the infinitive phrase is used as a modifier, double underline the word it modifies.

EX. __*N; DO*__ 1. Everyone wanted <u>to taste the punch</u>.

_____ 1. Darla wants to visit the Grand Ole Opry in Nashville.

_____ 2. Saul is the person to give your receipts to.

_____ 3. We went to the store to buy more pasta sauce.

_____ 4. Those people over there tried to talk to us about the movie.

_____ 5. To drive in the Indy 500 is Sallie's latest dream.

_____ 6. My great-grandfather once walked 40 miles to listen to Duke Ellington play.

_____ 7. Matthew thought it would be fun to get a crew cut.

_____ 8. Are you happy to be leaving tomorrow?

_____ 9. Cory designed the chair to fit at his new desk.

_____ 10. Aunt Jess gave us some money to buy a poster for our bedroom.

MODULE 3: THE PHRASE
APPOSITIVES AND APPOSITIVE PHRASES

3k An *appositive* is a noun or pronoun placed beside another noun or pronoun to identify or explain it.

EXAMPLES   Dad's brother, **Orville**, was named for one of the Wright brothers.

Ma Chan protested that she, a true **pacifist**, could never support a war.

3l An *appositive phrase* consists of an appositive and its modifiers.

EXAMPLES   The pigs, **three animals whose story is well known,** built three types of houses.

A people with both European and Native American ancestry, the Métis developed a unique culture.

EXERCISE 11   Identifying Appositives

Underline the appositive in each sentence below. Then double underline the word(s) the appositive identifies or explains.

EX.   <u>Katya</u>, my <u>friend</u>, is learning to speak Italian.

1. Those envelopes on the desk, the white ones, belong to Rafael.
2. Ms. Lin and Mr. Rinaldo, my favorite teachers, are planning a school musical for the spring.
3. Shanna will use pine, her favorite wood, to make that large picture frame.
4. Percy's solar energy science project, the first-place winner, will be on display in the school library today.
5. I am interested in learning more about Jesse Owens, the runner.
6. The new community center location, 6 Carlos Street, is near my grandmother's apartment.
7. My raincoat, the gray one in the closet, is new.
8. Our house guest, an expert on Cambodian history, will give a lecture today.
9. Have you ever tried tortellini soup, my specialty?
10. She bought a red carnation, her favorite flower.

EXERCISE 12   Identifying Appositive Phrases

Underline the appositive phrase in each sentence below. Then double underline the word(s) the appositive phrase identifies or explains.

EX.   <u>Akeem</u>, <u>a novice on the ice</u>, tried to stand up on his skates.

1. After the party, we proved to Dad that Shep, our new dog, can fetch a tennis ball from the creek.

2. Everyone at the show, over 200 people, loved Masie's new band.

3. Steven's stepfather, a former fighter pilot, now flies passenger planes for one of the major airlines.

4. Drew's sister, his company's cashier, moved to Maine, where she has a highly successful business.

5. Latoya actually has an appointment with a publisher to discuss her book, a novel called *The Life of a Sixteen-Year-Old.*

6. I can never get enough fresh corn, my favorite vegetable.

7. In the 1860s, some of my ancestors came to this country from Ireland, the "Emerald Isle."

8. My brother, the romantic, asked Ines to go with him to the dance.

9. If I had the money, I would like to own stock in that company, a lawn-furniture manufacturer.

10. The owners of the new theater, the largest in town, promise to sweep and wash the aisles after each screening.

11. Can you believe that my uncle, a professor at Tufts University, has published more than 150 articles?

12. The newspaper said that that auto dealer, the one with the crazy TV commercials, is running for mayor.

13. Ms. Lawson said she would have a party at the end of the year for our class, third-period English.

14. After I did my homework, 50 geometry problems, I helped my little brother make a snack.

15. Sara, Sue's cousin, and I found that we got along really well.

MODULE 3: THE PHRASE

MODULE REVIEW

A. Identifying Adjective and Adverb Phrases

In the sentences below, classify each italicized phrase. On the line before each sentence, write *ADJ* for *adjective phrase* or *ADV* for *adverb phrase*. Then double underline the word that the phrase modifies.

EX. __*ADV*__ The car <u>swerved</u> away *from the tree.*

_____ 1. A cup *of noodle soup* would make a nice lunch.

_____ 2. My friend Frieda walked carefully *around the stage.*

_____ 3. My arms were covered *with poison ivy.*

_____ 4. *During the blizzard,* we kept candles nearby.

_____ 5. Rena likes the view *from the fourth floor.*

_____ 6. The island *near the shore* attracts many tourists.

_____ 7. Luigi cleaned his room completely *except for his closet.*

_____ 8. My stamps are those *on the counter.*

_____ 9. The baby's forehead was warm *with a fever.*

_____ 10. Keith opened a can *of chickpeas.*

B. Classifying Verbal Phrases and Identifying Their Function

On the line before each sentence, classify the italicized phrase by writing *PP* for *participial phrase*, *GP* for *gerund phrase*, or *IP* for *infinitive phrase*. Then identify the phrase's function by writing *ADJ* for *adjective*, *ADV* for *adverb*, *DO* for *direct object*, *OP* for *object of a preposition*, *PN* for *predicate nominative*, or *S* for *subject*.

EX. __*IP; ADJ*__ It is time *to go to school.*

_____ 1. But I don't like *cleaning my room.*

_____ 2. *Peeking under the table,* Isaiah smiled at his dog.

_____ 3. After what Esperanza said, we tried *to encourage her.*

_____ 4. Because of the summer humidity, the clothes *stored in the garage* had mildewed.

_____ 5. Our goal is *to sell 50 boxes of cookies,* and we know it can be done if everyone contributes.

_____ 6. *Tanning too much* is now generally agreed to be unhealthy, especially for people with a history of skin problems.

_____ 7. The rules committee asked me *to remove some posters that my friends and I had put up.*

_____ 8. Besides driving at night in a storm, I also hate driving in heavy mist and fog.

_____ 9. Do you think that I like *waiting for the bus* any more than you do?

_____ 10. Is anyone here ready *to present his or her oral report today*?

C. Writing Sentences with Phrases

Write 10 sentences according to the following guidelines. Underline the italicized phrase given.

EX.   Use *after the show* as an adverb phrase.
      The director asked us to meet with her <u>after the show</u>.

1. Use *because of the festival* as an adverb phrase.

_____

2. Use *from Belgium* as an adjective phrase.

_____

3. Use *leaping over the fence* as a participial phrase.

_____

4. Use *moved from its usual spot* as a participial phrase.

_____

5. Use *replacing a flat tire* as a gerund phrase that is the object of a preposition.

_____

6. Use *applying for a job* as a gerund phrase that is the subject.

_____

7. Use *to taste* as an infinitive phrase that is a direct object.

_____

8. Use *to wear* as an infinitive phrase that is an adjective or an adverb.

_____

9. Use *to see the local rock band live* as an infinitive phrase that is a predicate nominative.

_____

10. Use *one of my teammates* as an appositive phrase.

_____

KINDS OF CLAUSES

4a An *independent* (or *main*) *clause* expresses a complete thought and can stand by itself as a sentence.

EXAMPLES **Mr. Yellowhair drove to Yuma.** [one independent clause]

Memdi turned the corner, but **Nara ran in the opposite direction.** [two independent clauses joined by a comma and a conjunction]

We picked up empty cans on our walk; we filled two 30-gallon trash bags. [two independent clauses joined by a semicolon]

Although the ground was bare, **we had a great time on our ski trip.** [one independent clause combined with a subordinate clause]

Usually, an independent clause by itself is called a sentence. It is called an independent clause when it is combined with at least one other clause (independent or subordinate) to form a sentence.

4b A *subordinate* (or *dependent*) *clause* does not express a complete thought and cannot stand alone as a sentence.

Subordinate means "less important." The meaning of a subordinate clause is complete only when the clause is attached to an independent clause. Words such as *whom, because,* or *that* usually signal the beginning of a subordinate clause.

EXAMPLES **whom** I introduced to Ms. Miltos
We had a visitor from Chicago **whom I introduced to Ms. Miltos**.

because Mom needed more space
Because Mom needed more space, we finally cleaned out the storage bin.

that she liked
Cam caught sight of a quilted jacket **that she liked** and pointed it out to Tran.

As the examples show, subordinate clauses can be located at the beginning, in the middle, or at the end of a sentence.

EXERCISE 1 Identifying Independent and Subordinate Clauses in Paragraphs

In the passage below, classify each italicized clause as either independent (*I*) or subordinate (*S*). Mark your answer above each italicized clause.

EX. Videogames, *which often attract negative commentary*, provide many surprising
      benefits.

[1] *Some people view videogames as a waste of time,* and some have even argued that the violence in videogames causes players to become more violent. [2] However, it's worth noting *that the research on this point is inconclusive.* [3] *While playing nonstop may have negative effects like reducing time for exercising and socializing,* gaming also has great potential benefits. [4] *Games can help students obtain scholarships,* practice perseverance, and relieve the negative effects of stress, depression, and more.

[5] Colleges across the U.S. have added Esports to their athletic programs and some offer scholarships for students *who perform well in tournaments.* [6] *While not every gamer will become famous from streaming on Twitch,* time spent playing games can still work in your favor. [7] *Difficult videogames create a level of grit and determination in players* that is difficult to replicate. [8] *When a player spends significant time trying and failing the same level with the intent to improve and eventually beat the level,* that player is unintentionally learning perseverance. [9] *Perseverance helps people face difficulties throughout life* and manage stress levels in everyday situations.

[10] Research at Texas A&M University found *that violent videogames helped students build coping mechanisms for relieving stress.* [11] *The University of London found* that the time spent playing games directly correlated to the amount of everyday stress people were able to relieve. [12] Gaming, *which can help older people with cognitive function,* also effectively treats depression, anxiety, post-traumatic stress disorder, and chronic pain.

[13] As researchers spend more time and resources discovering the effects of gaming, *players will have increasingly more options and more reasons to play.* [14] *Even if gaming isn't your preferred pastime,* you may find that its advantages can positively contribute to other goals or interests. [15] So the next time someone says you're wasting your time playing games, *you can tell them all of the benefits you're getting.*

MODULE 4: THE CLAUSE

THE ADJECTIVE CLAUSE

4c   An *adjective clause* is a subordinate clause that modifies a noun or a pronoun.

An adjective clause always follows the word or words it modifies and tells *which one* or *what kind*. An adjective clause is usually introduced by a ***relative pronoun***—a word that relates the clause to the word or words the clause modifies.

Relative Pronouns				
that	which	who	whom	whose

EXAMPLES   Primo chose the pumpkin **that was shaped like an egg**. [The adjective clause modifies the noun *pumpkin*, telling *which one*.]

The Pineyard Inn, **which has a small dining room**, served excellent Chinese food. [The adjective clause modifies the noun *Pineyard Inn*, telling *what kind* of restaurant.]

The man **who was president of the United States from 1977 to 1981** was born in Georgia. [The adjective clause modifies the noun *man*, telling *which one*.]

Sonia enjoyed the speech by Ms. Graham, **whom people called an expert in real estate**. [The adjective clause modifies the noun *Ms. Graham*, telling *which* person.]

Ms. Barkin, **whose dog frequently barks all night**, does not live far enough away. [The adjective clause modifies the noun *Ms. Barkin*, telling *which* person.]

An adjective clause may also begin with a relative adverb, such as *when* or *where*.

EXAMPLES   I began to wish for the day **when class would be over**.
Is the shop **where Kameko bought the wooden combs** in Kyoto?

The relative pronoun or relative adverb is sometimes not expressed, but its meaning is understood.

EXAMPLES   Can you look for the package **[that] you received last week**?
I can't recall the time **[when] we are supposed to catch the bus**.

EXERCISE 2   Identifying Adjective Clauses and the Words They Modify

In each sentence below, underline the adjective clause and circle the relative pronoun or relative adverb (or note the one that is understood). Then double underline the noun or pronoun that the clause modifies.

EX.   The <u>jack-o'-lantern</u> <u>that Von carved</u> is getting moldy.

1. Molly, who enjoys swimming, is going to Edgewater Beach.
2. Lincoln delivered his Gettysburg Address near a battlefield where thousands had died.
3. The eruption of Mount Vesuvius, which occurred in 79 CE, buried the city of Pompeii in lava.
4. This mahogany desk, which my stepfather built, has six drawers.
5. In November 1922, Howard Carter, who had been exploring for 25 years, discovered the tomb of King Tutankhamen.
6. Mr. Weiman will play the recording of the band concert that he conducted.
7. Keo is going to the auditorium where the honor society ceremony will be held.
8. Ms. Carlin spoke excitedly of the evening when she watched the eclipse.
9. Wilson enjoyed the film he saw last night.
10. Jody had the flu during the time the choir rehearsed the Slovenian song.

EXERCISE 3   Revising Sentences by Using Adjective Clauses

Revise each sentence below by adding an adjective clause.

EX.   The bicycle had lost a pedal.
       The bicycle that the boys were trying to sell had lost a pedal.

1. The bus departed from the station at noon.

   _____

2. Jacy used the red toothbrush.

   _____

3. The door led to the basement.

   _____

4. The baseball pitcher was elated.

   _____

5. Does the battery still have a charge?

   _____

6. Hira may sleep on the futon.

   _____

7. A large crowd gathered in the park.

   _____

8. Fran must fix a flat tire on the bicycle.

   _____

9. Enrique walked quickly to the store.

   _____

10. Joan enjoyed the stew.

   _____

4d An *adverb clause* is a subordinate clause that modifies a verb, an adjective, or an adverb.

An adverb clause tells *how*, *when*, *where*, *why*, *to what extent*, or *under what condition*.

EXAMPLES **If you need a subject for your essay**, start by reading the headlines on a news site. [The clause modifies the verb *start*, telling *under what condition*.]

That hamster seems happier **because we gave her a new wheel**. [The clause modifies the adjective *happier*, telling *why*.]

Sonia enjoys ice skating more **than her sister does**. [The clause modifies the adverb *more*, telling *to what extent*.]

An adverb clause that introduces a sentence is set off by a comma.

EXAMPLE **As soon as the sun shines,** the ice on the sidewalk will melt.

An adverb clause is introduced by a *subordinating conjunction*—a word that shows the relationship between the adverb clause and the word or words the clause modifies. Some subordinating conjunctions can also be used as prepositions.

Common Subordinating Conjunctions			
after	as though	since	when
although	because	so that	whenever
as	before	than	where
as if	how	though	wherever
as long as	if	unless	whether
as soon as	in order that	until	while

4e Part of a clause may be left out when the meaning can be understood from the context of the sentence. Such a clause is called an *elliptical clause*.

EXAMPLES Trish likes Jack White better **than [she likes] any other musician**.

When [you are] driving, you should be able to hear the traffic sounds and not just the radio.

EXERCISE 4   Identifying Adverb Clauses and the Words They Modify

In the following sentences, underline each adverb clause once. Then double underline the verb, adjective, or adverb that the clause modifies.

EX.   Dena arrived at school a half hour <u>sooner</u> <u>than her brother did</u>.

1. Although the work was not difficult, it took a long time.
2. The engine in your car should run smoothly unless there is below-zero weather.
3. You may use my bicycle as long as you take proper care of it.
4. The snow was deeper than anyone had ever seen it before.
5. We go to the movies whenever we hear about a worthwhile film.
6. While he waited for the bus, Turner practiced the song he was to perform later in the day.
7. For Kari, the exercises in yoga class were difficult because she had not tried them before.
8. The potato soup will be ready as soon as you add the spices.
9. Whenever her baby sister is asleep, Kim works on her research paper.
10. The rain fell steadily until our street became one enormous puddle.

EXERCISE 5   Writing Sentences with Adverb Clauses

Write five sentences by joining clauses from the list below. Use five different subordinating conjunctions from the chart in section 4d. Underline the adverb clauses once and the subordinating conjunctions twice.

a cold rain fell	the sun went down
the thread was worn	it was not a bitterly cold day
the jacket was not warm enough	the most difficult test was over
Nancy arrived at school early	the button fell off
she felt relieved	traffic was light

EX.   *<u>When a cold rain fell</u>, the jacket was not warm enough.*

1. _____

2. _____

3. _____

4. _____

5. _____

THE NOUN CLAUSE

4f A *noun clause* **is a subordinate clause used as a noun.**

A noun clause may be used as a subject, a predicate nominative, a direct object, an indirect object, or an object of a preposition.

SUBJECT	**Whatever you want to do** is all right with me.
PREDICATE NOMINATIVE	Home is **wherever I can cook a meal**.
DIRECT OBJECT	Kung doesn't know **whether he can join the team**.
INDIRECT OBJECT	The students handed **whoever walked by** a pamphlet.
OBJECT OF A PREPOSITION	No one could agree about **how the baby bird should be fed**.

Common Introductory Words for Noun Clauses				
Relative Pronouns				
that	whatever	whichever	whoever	whomever
what	which	who	whom	
Relative Adverbs				
how	when	where	whether	
if	whenever	wherever	why	

Sometimes the word that introduces a noun clause is not expressed.

EXAMPLE   I heard **[that] the class might travel to Baltimore in April**.

EXERCISE 6   Identifying and Classifying Noun Clauses

Underline the noun clause in each sentence. On the line before the sentence, identify the part of speech of the clause. Write *S* for *subject*, *PN* for *predicate nominative*, *DO* for *direct object*, *IO* for *indirect object*, or *OP* for *object of a preposition*.

EX.   _*DO*_   Sabrina wondered <u>which of the neighborhood dogs was barking</u>.

_____   1.   The mechanic described how an engine works.

_____   2.   Whichever piece Lawanda plays will be the highlight of the concert.

_____   3.   The question is whether we should rent bikes or use our own.

_____   4.   Pilar provided a copy of her resume to whomever she asked for a job.

_____   5.   The paint color was whatever my mother selected.

_____   6.   The apprentice does well what is assigned to her.

_____   7.   Whoever was awarded the prize must have been pleased.

_____ 8. On Saturday Joe will give whoever is interested a ride on his snowmobile.

_____ 9. Only the bus driver paid attention to where construction blocked traffic.

_____ 10. The speaker gave whoever heckled him a fast and funny answer.

_____ 11. How much students practice affects their playing ability.

_____ 12. You can order whatever is on the menu.

_____ 13. The banyan tree provides shade to whoever sits underneath it.

_____ 14. The mystery was which of the keys had been stolen and replaced.

_____ 15. Tanya brought whoever seemed interested a copy of her poem.

EXERCISE 7 Writing Sentences with Noun Clauses

Finish each sentence below by replacing the blank with a noun clause. Use the word in parentheses to introduce the noun clause. Write your completed sentences on your own paper.

EX. The rain washed away _____ . (Use *whatever*.)

The rain washed away whatever tracks the bear had left.

1. Put _____ at the front of the stage. (Use *whichever*.)

2. Mr. Ramírez agreed to sell _____ (Use *whatever*.)

3. _____ should switch off the lights. (Use *Whoever*.)

4. _____ pleases Ms. O'Toole greatly. (Use *That*.)

5. Mei Hua didn't know _____ (Use *whether*.)

6. I sent _____ a map and directions. (Use *whoever*.)

7. _____ need to leave class early. (Use *Whichever*.)

8. Nobody knows _____. (Use *when*.)

9. Mr. Hirata explained _____. (Use *why*.)

10. The mail carrier will deliver _____. (Use *whatever*.)

SENTENCE STRUCTURE

4g   According to their structure, sentences are classified as *simple*, *compound*, *complex*, or *compound-complex*.

(1) A *simple sentence* has one independent clause and no subordinate clauses.

EXAMPLES   Please turn down the volume for a moment.

Do you know another way out of town?

I could have walked even farther in these new shoes.

(2) A *compound sentence* has two or more independent clauses but no subordinate clauses.

Independent clauses may be joined by (1) a comma and a coordinating conjunction (*and*, *but*, *for*, *nor*, *or*, *so*, or *yet*); (2) by a semicolon; or (3) by a semicolon and a conjunctive adverb or transitional expression followed by a comma.

NOTE   *For* is used as a conjunction only if it connects independent clauses (usually in formal situations).

EXAMPLES   The Sherpas of Nepal are known as good mountaineers, **and** they often guide people in the Himalayas.

The park has occupied that corner since 1891; it was a popular gathering place in the 60s; now people seldom use it.

Tranh agreed to take the hen; **however,** he felt unhappy about the trade.

(3) A *complex sentence* has one independent clause and at least one subordinate clause.

EXAMPLES   The villagers thought **that dolls could draw disease out of a sick person**.

Although the Parks took us sightseeing, we stayed with the Kims **because they have an extra room**.

(4) A *compound-complex sentence* has two or more independent clauses and at least one subordinate clause.

EXAMPLES   Sequoyah created an alphabet **that has 86 symbols**; the Cherokee people still use it today.

After the bread rose, Meg punched it down, **and** Lily formed the dough into loaves.

EXERCISE 8   Classifying Sentences According to Structure

Identify the structure of each sentence below. On the line before the sentence, write *S* for *simple*, *C* for *compound*, *CX* for *complex*, and *CC* for *compound-complex*.

EX. *CX*   One of the most remarkable examples of multifamily housing that you can see on this continent is the cliff dwelling at Mesa Verde in southwestern Colorado.

_____ 1. The ancient structures of Mesa Verde give historians and tourists a glimpse into a fascinating culture.

_____ 2. Between 550 CE and the late 1300s, this area of southwestern Colorado was busy, but now the ancient buildings contain only memories.

_____ 3. Though the Anasazi were well known by other peoples in their own time, today relatively little is known about their way of life.

_____ 4. For about 750 years, the Anasazi lived and farmed on top of Mesa Verde.

_____ 5. The ancestors of the Anasazi were called Basket Makers; they perfected the art of making baskets that were both beautiful and useful.

_____ 6. Around 550 CE, some Basket Makers moved to Mesa Verde, where they developed a method of building dwellings called pithouses.

_____ 7. Soon the Anasazi learned to build square rooms with vertical walls, and their round pithouses were used only as ceremonial rooms.

_____ 8. Anasazi pottery has been found all over Mesa Verde; it is easily recognized by designs that were painted with black paint in intricate lines, squares, and other geometric shapes.

_____ 9. Because the plateaus usually received enough rain, the Anasazi managed to grow corn, beans, and squash.

_____ 10. Thousands of Anasazi lived in cliff dwellings of Mesa Verde until the late 1300s, when they mysteriously abandoned their homes.

MODULE 4: THE CLAUSE
SENTENCE PURPOSE

4h   Sentences are classified according to purpose as *declarative*, *imperative*, *interrogative*, or *exclamatory*.

(1) A *declarative sentence* makes a statement. All declarative sentences end with periods.

EXAMPLE   Children in Great Britain celebrate Guy Fawkes Day with bonfires and fireworks.

(2) An *imperative sentence* gives a command or makes a request. Imperative sentences usually end with periods, but a very strong command may end with an exclamation point.

EXAMPLES   First, take the pine needles out of your basket.
Run for the hills!

(3) An *interrogative sentence* asks a question. Interrogative sentences end with question marks.

EXAMPLES   Do you keep spoke wrenches in stock?
Where are those T-shirts with the school's name on them?

NOTE   Any sentence may be spoken in such a way that it is interrogative. If so, the sentence should end with a question mark.

EXAMPLE   You called me?

(4) An *exclamatory sentence* expresses strong feeling. Exclamatory sentences end with exclamation points.

EXAMPLES   Faye is such a good singer!
You look so glamorous!

NOTE   Any sentence may be spoken in such a way that it is exclamatory. If so, the sentence should end with an exclamation point.

EXAMPLE   What happened to all of the apples!

EXERCISE 9 Classifying Sentences According to Purpose

Identify the purpose of each sentence. On the line before the sentence, write *D* for *declarative*, *IMP* for *imperative*, *INT* for *interrogative*, or *E* for *exclamatory*. Also add the correct end marks.

EX. __*D*__ I read this book of fairy tales when I was very young.

_____ 1. At 10:00 p.m., the last train will leave the station

_____ 2. How many hours will Latoya need to bake enough bread for everyone

_____ 3. In certain parts of the tropics, it usually rains every day, but only for a short period of time

_____ 4. Those two cats curl up together when they're cold

_____ 5. Get this lawn mowed today

_____ 6. How quickly can you do your homework and still answer all the problems correctly

_____ 7. I won't be able to see my friends again for six full weeks

_____ 8. The program for tonight's concert has been changed

_____ 9. Chung Sook enjoys the institute so much that he plans to take additional courses

_____ 10. Is it necessary to soak the beans overnight before we cook them

_____ 11. That buzzing sound is so annoying

_____ 12. Are all of the children who are going on the field trip here yet

_____ 13. Write to your U.S. senator about your views on the recycling issue

_____ 14. Watch out for the icy steps

_____ 15. When was the last time you practiced your trumpet

_____ 16. After the festival, Charlie and Sloan walked home together

_____ 17. How is it that you have never met him before

_____ 18. Do the dishes as soon as you finish eating

_____ 19. Tell me how long it takes you to peel a potato

_____ 20. Yuck, that shirt is a mess

MODULE 4: THE CLAUSE
MODULE REVIEW

A. Identifying Independent and Subordinate Clauses

Classify the italicized clause in each sentence below. On the line before the sentence, write *I* for *independent clause*, *ADJ* for *adjective clause*, *ADV* for *adverb clause*, or *N* for *noun clause*.

EX. ___*A*___ Nels paused and stared at the sky, *which had suddenly darkened.*

_____ 1. *Kenya*, a country on the east coast of Africa, *became independent in 1963.*

_____ 2. Vo, *whose hair was still uncombed*, went out to collect the newspaper from the lawn.

_____ 3. *What I learned in school today* will be of use when I go to take my driver's license exam.

_____ 4. Sarah left for school *after Molly came home from her morning run.*

_____ 5. *Although nothing could have warned him of the danger*, Angelo suddenly moved off in another direction.

_____ 6. A short but fascinating story is *how Franklin won the election.*

_____ 7. Len emerged briefly from the shade *in which he had been running* into bright sunlight.

_____ 8. *The kiwi bird lives in New Zealand, has wings, but cannot fly.*

_____ 9. *Whoever moves fastest* will become our starting forward.

_____ 10. Mrs. Fung is reading her daughter's favorite book, the one about mothers *who were brought up in traditional ways* and their very modern daughters.

B.   Identifying Sentences by Structure and Purpose

Identify the structure of each sentence. On the line before the sentence, write *S* for *simple*, *CD* for *compound*, *CX* for *complex*, and *CC* for *compound-complex*. Then identify the purpose of each sentence. Write *D* for *declarative*, *IMP* for *imperative*, *INT* for *interrogative*, or *E* for *exclamatory*.

EX.   <u>*CX; IMP*</u>   While exiting a building during a fire drill, do not talk with other students.

_____   1. The 2018 Winter Olympic Games were held in Pyeongchang, South Korea.

_____   2. Once they had their grandmother's approval, Elena stripped the old paint from the chair, and Diane sanded the surface.

_____   3. Does a kitten, unless it is taught, know how to hunt?

_____   4. Read the module; then respond to questions 1 through 15.

_____   5. Some of the planets have moons, and one of the planets has rings; can you identify all of these planets?

_____   6. If Tisa does one hundred pushups, I'll be amazed!

_____   7. Roald Amundsen was a courageous explorer and became the first man to reach the South Pole.

_____   8. Even if we're losing by 60 points, don't even think of quitting the game!

_____   9. If the plumber cleaned out the drain, why can't we use the sink?

_____   10. Mindy wants to shop for sweaters, and Cao must buy a new jacket before the weather turns cold.

C. Using Clauses to Write a Poem

Create a poem by filling in each line below. Use and label at least one adverb clause, one adjective clause, and one noun clause.

EX.   I believe *that I have a purpose*. (*noun cl.*)

Today

I believe _____.

I dream _____.

I want _____.

I fear _____.

Yesterday

I learned much _____.

When _____ I stayed silent.

The people _____ didn't hear me.

But _____.

Tomorrow

If _____ I will succeed with my plans.

I will _____ because _____.

Listen to _____.

You _____.

MODULE 5: AGREEMENT
SUBJECT-VERB AGREEMENT

Number is the form of a word that indicates whether the word is singular or plural.

5a   A word that refers to one person or thing is *singular* in number. A word that refers to more than one is *plural* in number.

SINGULAR	employer	theory	woman	that	either	it
PLURAL	employers	theories	women	those	both	they

Most nouns that end in *s* are plural; most present-tense verbs that end in *s* are singular. Past-tense verbs (except *be*) have the same form in both the singular and the plural.

NOTE   The singular pronouns *I* and *you* almost always take plural verbs.
The only exceptions are the forms *I am* and *I was*.

5b   A verb should agree with its subject in number.

(1) Singular subjects take singular verbs.

EXAMPLE   The falcon **flies** above the rabbit warren. [The singular verb *flies* agrees with the singular subject *falcon*.]

(2) Plural subjects take plural verbs.

EXAMPLE   The falcons **fly** above the rabbit warren. [The plural verb *fly* agrees with the plural subject *falcons*.]

Like the one-word verb in each of the preceding examples, a verb phrase must also agree in number with its subject. The number of a verb phrase is indicated by the form of its first auxiliary (helping) verb.

EXAMPLES   My aunt **is rebuilding** a classic Thunderbird. [singular subject and verb phrase]
My aunts **are rebuilding** a classic Thunderbird. [plural subject and verb phrase]

EXERCISE 1   Selecting Verbs That Agree in Number with Their Subjects

For each of the following phrases, underline the verb or verb phrase in parentheses that agrees in number with its subject.

EX.   she (*run, runs*)

1. horse (*gallops, gallop*)
2. roses (*blooms, bloom*)
3. fans (*is shouting, are shouting*)
4. candidate (*announces, announce*)
5. Rachel (*is practicing, are practicing*)
6. chefs (*slices, slice*)
7. we (*decides, decide*)
8. judge (*hears, hear*)
9. fingers (*flexes, flex*)
10. elephant (*is charging, are charging*)
11. skyscrapers (*towers, tower*)
12. gazelles (*leaps, leap*)
13. cookies (*is crumbling, are crumbling*)
14. helicopter (*hovers, hover*)
15. reporter (*is waiting, are waiting*)
16. radio signals (*carries, carry*)
17. water (*boils, boil*)
18. students (*is uniting, are uniting*)
19. performer (*dazzles, dazzle*)
20. Carlos (*forgets, forget*)

EXERCISE 2   Identifying Subjects and Verbs That Agree in Number

For each sentence below, underline the verb or verb phrase in parentheses that agrees in number with its subject.

EX.   Athletes (*trains, <u>train</u>*) rigorously for the demanding triathlon.

1. The oceanographers (*is collecting, are collecting*) samples of algae.
2. Every year, several million tourists (*visits, visit*) Europe.
3. Alaska (*covers, cover*) the most area of any state in the United States.
4. Ellie (*maneuvers, maneuver*) the bike down the path expertly.
5. The interpreter (*translates, translate*) the ambassador's speech.
6. Julia (*is refinishing, are refinishing*) the woodwork on the antique dresser.
7. The computer program (*alphabetizes, alphabetize*) automatically.
8. In our school, many students (*speaks, speak*) more than one language.
9. The cultural festival (*has, have*) crafts from over 10 countries.
10. Storm clouds (*is gathering, are gathering*) above the plain.
11. The acrobats (*is performing, are performing*) on Saturday.
12. The accountant (*is totaling, are totaling*) the figures.
13. Bees (*plays, play*) a vital role in the pollination of flowers.
14. We (*collects, collect*) cans for recycling.
15. The librarians (*is shelving, are shelving*) the new books.
16. The Rio Grande (*marks, mark*) the border between Texas and Mexico.
17. Keiko (*is throwing, are throwing*) a surprise party for her sister.
18. The museum (*is holding, are holding*) a special exhibit on Chinese textiles.
19. The orioles (*is nesting, are nesting*) outside the kitchen window.
20. Our teachers (*urges, urge*) us to read the material twice.

5c **The number of the subject is not changed by a phrase or a clause following the subject.**

EXAMPLES The **boxes are** filled with videotapes.

The **boxes** under the bed **are** filled with videotapes. [The prepositional phrase *under the bed* does not affect the number of the subject *boxes*.]

Leonard Bernstein earned fame as a composer.

Leonard Bernstein, one of this country's most noted conductors, **earned** fame as a composer. [The appositive phrase *one of this country's most noted conductors* does not affect the number of the subject *Leonard Bernstein*.]

The **jerseys are** purple, yellow, and black.

The **jerseys** that we ordered **are** purple, yellow, and black. [The adjective clause *that we ordered* does not affect the number of the subject *jerseys*.]

A prepositional phrase may begin with a ***compound preposition*** such as *together with, in addition to, as well as,* or *along with*. These phrases do not affect the number of the verb.

EXAMPLES **Lanny**, as well as his brother, **is planning** a trip.[singular subject and verb]

Your **socks**, along with your hat, **are** in the closet.[plural subject and verb]

EXERCISE 3   Identifying Subjects and Verbs That Agree in Number

For each of the following sentences, underline the verb or verb phrase in parentheses that agrees in number with its subject.

EX. The package that I sent (<u>*contains*</u>, *contain*) the information.

1. Mr. Delgado, one of my coworkers, (*bakes, bake*) his own bread.

2. The bins for the clothing drive (*is filling, are filling*) quickly.

3. Rice, as well as pasta, (*is, are*) a good source of complex carbohydrates.

4. The books on the bottom shelf (*is, are*) oversized.

5. Many houses along the river (*was, were*) damaged by the flood.

6. Our next-door neighbors (*plants, plant*) bulbs in their garden.

7. George Washington, the first president of the United States, (*is, are*) known as a founding father.

8. The jets that just landed (needs, need) refueling.

9. Raisins, together with granola, (*makes, make*) trail mix.

10. The students who attended the meeting (*supports, support*) the school board's new policies.

EXERCISE 4   Proofreading a Paragraph for Subject-Verb Agreement

In the paragraph below, draw a line through each verb or verb phrase that does not agree with its subject. Write the correct form of the verb or verb phrase in the space above the error. If a sentence contains no errors, write *C* above it.

        is
EX.   The floor ~~are~~ a central part of Japanese houses.

[1] For thousands of years, the floor have been the center of activity in Japanese houses. [2] Sitting, as well as sleeping, are done on the floor. [3] A *tatami* are the floor covering used in Japanese housing. [4] These rectangular mats is made from rice straw. [5] A typical *tatami* measure about six feet by three feet and is two inches thick. [6] In some houses space are left between the mats. [7] In others, the mats completely covers the floor. [8] People take off their shoes at the door to protect the floor and the mats. [9] The foot covering that they put on are called a *tabi*, which is like a slipper. [10] The regular size of the *tatami* have greatly influenced Japanese architecture. [11] The height of *shoji*, which are sliding doors, match the length of the *tatami*. [12] A *toko-no-ma*, an area for displaying art, are also influenced by the *tatami*. [13] The *toko-no-ma* is positioned at eye-level of a person sitting on a *tatami*. [14] A person often describe a room by the number of mats that cover the floor. [15] For example, a six-mat room is a room whose floor is covered by six *tatami*.

MODULE 5: AGREEMENT

AGREEMENT WITH INDEFINITE PRONOUNS

5d   The following indefinite pronouns are singular: *anybody, anyone, anything, each, either, everybody, everyone, everything, neither, nobody, no one, nothing, one, somebody, someone,* and *something.* A singular indefinite pronoun takes a singular verb.

EXAMPLES   **Each** of you **is** my friend. [singular subject, singular verb]

Everything he does **is** a success. [singular subject, singular verb]

No one who has seen the show **says** it is worth 50 dollars a ticket. [singular subject, singular verb]

5e   The following indefinite pronouns are plural: *both, few, many,* and *several.* A plural indefinite pronoun takes a plural verb.

EXAMPLES   **Both** of my aunts **say** they will vote. [plural subject, plural verb]

Many in my neighborhood **are** complaining about the drought. [plural subject, plural verb]

5f   The following indefinite pronouns may be either singular or plural: *all, any, most, none,* and *some.*

These pronouns are singular when they refer to a singular word and are plural when they refer to plural words.

EXAMPLES   **Most** of the river **runs** through the Great Plains. [*Most* refers to the singular noun *river.*]

Most of the windows **are** open. [*Most* refers to the plural noun *windows.*]

Some of the wharf **was** rebuilt after the hurricane. [*Some* refers to the singular noun *wharf.*]

Some of the stores **offer** student discounts. [*Some* refers to the plural noun *stores.*]

NOTE   The word *none* is singular when it means "not one" and plural when it means "not any."

EXAMPLES   **None** of the spots **shows**. [*Not one* shows.]

None of the spots **show**. [*Not any* show.]

EXERCISE 5   Identifying Subjects and Verbs That Agree in Number

For each of the following sentences, underline the verb or verb phrase in parentheses that agrees in number with its subject.

    EX. Everyone who waited in line (*was, were*) able to buy tickets.

1. Both of the songs (*sounds, sound*) familiar.
2. Some of the broccoli (*needs, need*) to be defrosted.
3. For tryouts, each of the actors (*prepares, prepare*) an audition piece.
4. Most of the classes (*has, have*) small enrollments.
5. Neither of the restaurants (*accepts, accept*) reservations.
6. Each thread in the tapestry (*is, are*) made of handspun silk.
7. Someone in the bleachers (*is waving, are waving*) to you.
8. Some of the runners (*looks, look*) tired.
9. Any of the dresses (*is, are*) appropriate for the occasion.
10. Some of the trains (*runs, run*) on weekends.
11. Both of the online newspapers (*offers, offer*) excellent local news coverage.
12. Some of my sources (*is, are*) firsthand.
13. All of the meteorologists (*is predicting, are predicting*) a severe thunderstorm.
14. Most of my colleagues (*attends, attend*) the conference.
15. None of the defendant's alibis (*holds, hold*) up in court.
16. Everyone who reads the book (*has, have*) a different interpretation.
17. Most of Siri's arguments (*makes, make*) sense.
18. Many of the diners (*orders, order*) the vegetarian chili.
19. One of the artists (*incorporates, incorporate*) recycled materials into her paintings.
20. Most of the council members (*votes, vote*) on the proposal.
21. Many at the airport (*is experiencing, are experiencing*) travel delays.
22. Everyone (*understands, understand*) the director's instructions.
23. Either of your plans (*is, are*) acceptable.
24. Anyone who wants to attend (*is, are*) welcome.
25. No one (*wants, want*) the festival to end.

THE COMPOUND SUBJECT

A *compound subject* consists of two or more nouns or pronouns that are joined by a conjunction and have the same verb.

5g   Subjects joined by *and* usually take a plural verb.

(1) Compound subjects joined by *and* that name more than one person or thing always take plural verbs.

EXAMPLES   **Doug** and **Mika met** at Bruno's party.

Corn, **wheat**, and **soybeans are** that country's main crops.

(2) Compound subjects joined by *and* that name only one person or one thing take a singular verb.

EXAMPLES   My best **friend** and **tutor is** Devon. [one person]

Red beans and **rice is** a staple at our house. [one thing]

5h   Singular subjects joined by *or* or *nor* take a singular verb.

EXAMPLES   Either **he** or **Kathie needs** to stay here.

Neither **Spike** nor **Brandy** ever **wears** a sweater.

5i   When a singular subject and a plural subject are joined by *or* or *nor*, the verb agrees with the subject nearer the verb.

EXAMPLES   Either my **sister** or my **cousins are going** to pick you up. [The plural subject *cousins* is nearer the verb.]

Either my **cousins** or my **sister is going** to pick you up. [The singular subject *sister* is nearer the verb.]

EXERCISE 6   Correcting Errors in Subject-Verb Agreement

In the following sentences, draw a line through each verb that does not agree in number with its subject. Write the correct form of the verb in the space above the error. If a sentence contains no agreement errors, write *C* above it.

enjoy
EX.   Both Damon and Krista ~~enjoys~~ jazz music.

1. Law and order were the main theme of the mayoral campaign.

2. Bicycling and in-line skating is enjoyable and healthy forms of exercise.

3. Sandra and her cousins sees each other every year at their family reunion.

4. The project head and computer analyst are my aunt.

5. Neither Nicole nor Tracy takes credit for the rally's success.

6. Your sister and your mother looks alike.

7. Mushrooms and zucchini is my favorite vegetables.

8. Either my father or I usually makes dinner.

9. Neither my swimming coach nor my history teacher know Ms. Kim.

10. The ode and the sonnet is forms of poetry.

11. Firsthand accounts and historical evidence supports the archeologist's claim.

12. Either the director or the committee members schedules the meeting.

13. Margo and Brian is learning Japanese.

14. Dogs and wolves belongs to the canine family.

15. Crackers and milk are my favorite snack.

16. Neither palm trees nor cactuses grows in northern climates.

17. James Baldwin and Ralph Ellison were two of the writers Tom wrote about in his English paper.

18. Hot peppers and curry powder makes the dish very hot.

19. Either Josh or Anthony bat after the shortstop.

20. Neither the Senate nor the House of Representatives is in session.

EXERCISE 7 Using Verbs That Agree in Number with Compound Subjects

Write five sentences about your family history. In each sentence, use a compound subject joined by *and*, *or*, or *nor*. Include one example of two singular subjects joined by *either/or* or *neither/nor* and one singular and one plural subject joined by *either/or* or *neither/nor*. Pay special attention to subject-verb agreement.

EX.   *My Shawnee heritage and my Irish heritage are very special to my family.*

_____

_____

_____

_____

_____

COLLECTIVE NOUNS

5j   Collective nouns may be either singular or plural.

A *collective noun* is singular in form, but it names a group of persons or things.

Common Collective Nouns			
alliance	club	flock	group
army	committee	group	public
assembly	crowd	herd	staff
audience	club	jury	team
band	family	majority	troop
class	club	panel	

Use a plural verb when the noun refers to the members of the group as individuals. Use a singular verb with a collective noun when the noun refers to the group as a unit.

EXAMPLES   The band **is** unwilling to play an encore.
            The band **disagree** about what song to play next.

EXERCISE 8   Writing Sentences with Collective Nouns

From the chart above, select five collective nouns. Write a pair of sentences using each noun. Each pair should show how the collective noun may be either singular or plural.

> EX. *a. The jury finds the defendant not guilty.*
>   *b. The jury disagree on how the defendant should be compensated.*

1. a. _____
   b. _____
2. a. _____
   b. _____
3. a. _____
   b. _____
4. a. _____
   b. _____
5. a. _____
   b. _____

A.   Identifying Correct Verbs in Sentences

In each of the sentences below, underline the verb or verb phrase in parentheses that agrees in number with its subject.

EX.   Those olives (*is, <u>are</u>*) extremely salty.

1. Many of my friends (*studies, study*) together before exams.
2. The flamenco dancers (*is wearing, are wearing*) authentic costumes.
3. Nuna, one of the researchers, (*dedicates, dedicate*) herself to her job.
4. Centimeters and decimeters (*is, are*) metric units of measurement.
5. My sister, as well as my parents, (*shares, share*) my enthusiasm.
6. Some of the buildings (*is, are*) visible through the fog.
7. The class (*assigns, assign*) responsibilities to different groups of students.
8. Neither Réka nor Emilio (*wants, want*) to leave.
9. Rhythm and blues (*is, are*) Carla's favorite type of music.
10. The doctor (*is expecting, are expecting*) your visit.

B.   Making Verbs Agree with Their Subjects

In each sentence below, draw a line through any verb that does not agree in number with its subject. Then, on the line before the sentence, write the correct form of the verb. If a sentence contains no errors, write *C*.

EX.   ___*needs*___   Each of the potatoes ~~need~~ to be peeled.

_____ 1. A swarm of bees are heading toward the hive.
_____ 2. Many of the younger campers miss their parents.
_____ 3. Wax from the candles are dripping on the table.
_____ 4. Either the magician or the band provide the entertainment.
_____ 5. "The song that we heard remind me of summer," said Jill.
_____ 6. Both of those articles reports on recent fundraising events.
_____ 7. Confidence and determination is important qualities.
_____ 8. Some species of bamboo grows nearly three feet a day.
_____ 9. The magazine, along with the journals, have arrived.
_____ 10. Most of the shops in this area offer discounts on seasonal items.

OTHER PROBLEMS IN AGREEMENT

5k   A verb agrees with its subject, not with its predicate nominative.

EXAMPLES   **Science labs are** my favorite school activity. [plural subject, plural verb]

My favorite school activity is science labs. [singular subject, singular verb]

5l   A subject preceded by *every* or *many a/an* takes a singular verb.

EXAMPLES   **Every** new day **promises** something new.
Many a day **has** passed since I sent her that letter.

5m   An expression stating an amount may be singular or plural.

(1) An expression stating an amount is singular when the amount is thought of as a unit and is plural when the amount is thought of as many parts.

EXAMPLES   If you ask me, **six cars is** a caravan. [The *cars* are thought of as a unit.]

Six cars are leaving from school for Memphis later this afternoon. [The *cars* are thought of separately.]

(2) A fraction or a percentage is singular when it refers to a singular word and plural when it refers to a plural word.

EXAMPLES   **Three-fourths** of the committee **is** a quorum. [The percentage refers to the singular noun *committee*.]

Three-fourths of the committee members **are** present. [The percentage refers to the plural noun *members*.]

Seventy percent of the student body **agrees** with the decision. [The percentage refers to the singular noun *body*.]

Seventy percent of the students **agree** with the decision. [The percentage refers to the plural noun *students*.]

(3) Expressions of measurement (length, weight, capacity, area) are usually singular.

EXAMPLE   **Eight hundred meters is** a long way to run.

5n   The title of a creative work (such as a book, song, film, or painting) or the name of a country (even if it is plural in form) takes a singular verb.

EXAMPLES   Louisa May Alcott's ***Little Women* was** largely autobiographical.
The United States elects its president every leap year.

5o Many nouns that are plural in form are singular in meaning.

(1) The following nouns always take singular verbs.

civics	genetics	news
economics	mathematics	physics
electronics	linguistics	

EXAMPLE **Civics is** more than just the study of the law.

(2) The following nouns always take plural verbs.

binoculars   pliers   shears   trousers   eyeglasses   scissors

EXAMPLE My **eyeglasses are** no longer strong enough.

(3) The name of an organization (even if it is plural in form) usually takes a singular verb.

EXAMPLES **General Motors is** a large company.
The United Nations is composed primarily of the General Assembly and the Security Council.

(4) Many nouns ending in *-ics*, such as *acoustics, athletics, ethics, politics, statistics,* and *tactics,* may be singular or plural.

EXAMPLES **Politics is** what I plan to study in college.
My **politics are** similar to my parents'.

5p In the expression *number of*, the word *number* is singular when preceded by *the* and is plural when preceded by *a*.

EXAMPLES **The number of** pets in our building **has skyrocketed**.
A number of people **have** acquired them recently.

5q When the subject follows the verb, as in questions and in sentences beginning with *here* and *there*, identify the subject and make sure that the verb agrees with it.

The verb usually comes before the subject in sentences beginning with *Here* or *There* and in questions.

EXAMPLES Here **is** the **flower** you brought.
Here **are** the **flowers** you brought.

There **was** a **horse** in the field.
There **were** no **horses** in the field.

When **is your brother** coming to visit?
When **are your brothers** coming to visit?

NOTE   Contractions such as *Here's*, *There's*, *When's*, and *Where's* incorporate the verb *is*. Use such contractions only with subjects that are singular in meaning.

    INCORRECT   When's your classes?
      CORRECT   When **are** your **classes**?

    INCORRECT   Here's my new shoes.
      CORRECT   Here **are** my new **shoes**.
      CORRECT   Here's my new **pair** of shoes.

5r   When a relative pronoun (*that, which,* or *who*) is the subject of an adjective clause, the verb in the clause agrees with the word to which the relative pronoun refers.

EXAMPLES   My yoga class, **which meets** on Monday, is scheduling an extra session. [*Which* refers to the singular noun *class*.]
          I know people **who design** clothes. [*Who* refers to the plural noun *people*.]

NOTE   A relative pronoun takes a plural verb when its antecedent is preceded by *one of those* or *one of these*. When its antecedent is preceded by *the only one of those* (or *these*), the relative pronoun takes a singular verb.

    EXAMPLES   Ursula is **one of those runners who are** on both the cross-country and the track teams.
          The portrait over the fireplace is **the only one of those paintings that is** not by my father.

EXERCISE 9   Selecting Verbs That Agree in Number with Their Subjects

In each of the following sentences, underline the verb or contraction in parentheses that agrees in number with its subject.

   EX.   Where (*is, <u>are</u>*) the pliers?

1. Sore muscles (*is, are*) the first sign that I have exercised too hard.
2. Many a president (*has, have*) sat in this room.
3. There (*is, are*) nine players on a baseball team.
4. The Peace Corps (*is, are*) headquartered in Washington, DC.
5. The city hall is the only one of those buildings that (*is, are*) scheduled for demolition.
6. The number of mosquitoes (*has, have*) decreased this month.

7. *One Writer's Beginnings* (*is, are*) Eudora Welty's account of growing up in Jackson, Mississippi.

8. Five percent of the crop (*was, were*) affected by the frost.

9. "My goal (*is, are*) increased sales and salary increases," the manager announced.

10. Mathematics (*has, have*) always been Charlotte's best subject.

EXERCISE 10 Proofreading a Paragraph for Subject-Verb Agreement

In the paragraph below, draw a line through any verb or verb phrase that does not agree in number with its subject. Write the correct form of the verb in the space above the incorrect word. If a sentence contains no agreement errors, write *C*.

EX. Jacqueline Cochran's (1906–1980) career and achievements ~~is~~ *are* outstanding.

[1] After Cochran learned to fly in 1932, every speed, distance, and altitude record were hers to break. [2] It was her record-breaking abilities and her gender that brought her fame. [3] Two air-speed records was set in 1938, one of them by Cochran. [4] Military service and working as a pilot instructor was another part of Cochran's success. [5] A number of female pilots was trained by Cochran during the war. [6] The Women's Air Force Service Pilots were the organization that Cochran headed in 1943. [7] Many a flying record were broken by the skilled pilot in the years that followed. [8] Flying faster than the speed of sound and flying twice the speed of sound was among Cochran's many firsts. [9] Another first for a woman, 1,429 miles per hour were the speed record Cochran set in 1964. [10] Aeronautics owe a great deal to Jacqueline Cochran.

MODULE 5: AGREEMENT
REVIEW EXERCISE 2

A.   Identifying Verbs That Agree in Number with Their Subjects

In each sentence below, underline the verb or contraction that agrees in number with its subject.

EX.   Where (*is, are*) the reference materials?

1. Phonetics (*is, are*) the subject of today's discussion.

2. Nearly three-fourths of Earth's surface (*is, are*) covered by water.

3. This is one of those companies that (*leads, lead*) tours of the Grand Canyon.

4. Ravi's trousers (*needs, need*) to be hemmed.

5. The United Auto Workers (*is, are*) a powerful union.

6. The debate club's ethics (*is, are*) always honorable.

7. Those two singers (*is, are*) performing a duet.

8. The new shears (*makes, make*) trimming the bushes much easier.

9. Traveling 10 miles by car (*is, are*) not a long distance.

10. Jogging and reading (*is, are*) what I do to relax.

11. The Netherlands (*observes, observe*) a national holiday on April 30.

12. Only 30 percent of the renovation (*remains, remain*) to be finished.

13. Those sea lions, which live off the California coast, (*has, have*) been thriving.

14. What (*is, are*) the organization's policies?

15. The United States (*ranks, rank*) third in population among countries.

16. News from the battlefield (*was, were*) encouraging.

17. A number of the applications that (*was, were*) submitted for the job opening interested the director.

18. Vivaldi's *Four Seasons* (*is, are*) being performed by the Boston Symphony Orchestra.

19. What the documentary reveals (*is, are*) corruption and criminal activity.

20. Four boxes (*is, are*) inside the crate.

B. Proofreading a Paragraph for Errors in Subject-Verb Agreement

In the paragraphs below, draw a line through any verb or verb phrase that does not agree in number with its subject. Write the correct form of the verb in the space above the incorrect word. If a sentence contains no agreement errors, write *C* above it.

EX. Architect I. M. Pei (1917–2019) has designed buildings with a sense of beauty

        pleases

that ~~please~~ museum-goers around the world.

[1] A number of public buildings in the United States, France, and China has been designed by Pei. [2] Although Pei was born in China in 1917, the United States were home to the architect since 1935. [3] His bold designs for museums in Washington, DC and Paris made Pei famous. [4] In 1978, Pei designed the East Building of Washington's National Gallery of Art. [5] When visitors enter the gallery, they sees a large triangular space and a small number of paintings. [6] Pei's use of open space and light leave a lasting impression.

[7] Paris's Louvre Museum celebrated its bicentennial in 1993 with the opening of a newly renovated wing. [8] One billion dollars were the price tag for the renovation, headed by Pei. [9] Two-thirds of the renovation were completed in time for the bicentennial celebration. [10] Three courtyards was renovated in the Richelieu Wing. [11] Enormous skylights was Pei's trademark, and Pei installed them over each courtyard. [12] The 90 feet of space between the floors and paned ceilings bring light to the once dim halls. [13] The 22,000 square meters gained by the renovation are twice the old exhibition space. [14] These statistics suggest that the renovation was both practical and pleasing. [15] Since the renovation, many a visitor have passed through Pei's glass pyramid, which serves as the museum's entrance.

MODULE 5: AGREEMENT

PRONOUN AGREEMENT

A pronoun usually refers to a noun or another pronoun. The word to which a pronoun refers is called its ***antecedent***. The ***number*** of a noun or pronoun is either *singular* or *plural*.

5s   A pronoun should agree with its antecedent in number and in gender.

(1) Use a singular pronoun to refer to a singular antecedent; use a plural pronoun to refer to a plural antecedent.

EXAMPLES   **Esperanza** sold **her** bicycle to buy in-line skates. [The singular pronoun *her* refers to the singular antecedent *Esperanza*.]

Before I was born, **the Dodgers and the Giants** moved **their** teams to California. [The plural pronoun *their* refers to the plural antecedent *the Dodgers and the Giants*.]

The ***gender*** of a singular noun or pronoun is either *masculine, feminine*, or *neuter* (neither masculine nor feminine).

(2) The singular pronouns *he, him, his,* and *himself* refer to masculine antecedents. The singular pronouns *she, her, hers,* and *herself* refer to feminine antecedents. The singular pronouns *it, its,* and *itself* refer to antecedents that are neuter.

EXAMPLES   **Watson** built this model of the Golden Gate bridge **himself**. [The masculine pronoun *himself* refers to the masculine antecedent *Watson*.]

Ruby knew the blue ribbon would be **hers**. [The feminine pronoun *hers* refers to the feminine antecedent *Ruby*.]

After years of use, the **table** had lost **its** shine. [The neuter pronoun *its* refers to the neuter antecedent *table*.]

If a singular antecedent may be either masculine or feminine, use both the masculine and feminine pronouns to refer to it.

EXAMPLES   **Anyone** who is going on the trip should bring **his or her** sketchbook.
Everybody who saw the trick tried to do it **himself or herself**.

Often, you can avoid the "his or her" construction by revising the sentence, using the plural forms of both the pronoun and its antecedent.

EXAMPLES   **All** of the persons going on the trip should bring **their** sketchbooks.
All of those who saw the trick tried to do it **themselves**.

5t   Use a singular pronoun to refer to the following antecedents: *anybody, anyone, each, either, everybody, everyone, neither, nobody, no one, one, somebody,* and *someone.*

These words do not indicate gender. To determine their gender, look at the phrases following them.

EXAMPLES   **Each** of the **girls** has worn **her** cap.
One of the **men** forgot **his** wallet.

5u   Use a singular pronoun to refer to two or more singular antecedents joined by *or* or *nor.*

EXAMPLES   **Either Mitchell or Marcel** promised to bring **his** amplifier.
Neither Grace nor Ludmilla said **she** knew how far it was to Sacramento.

5v   Use a plural pronoun to refer to two or more singular antecedents joined by *and.*

EXAMPLES   If you see **Luca and Troy**, tell **them** Ms. Yamamoto wants **them** to come to her office.
Carl, **Antonia**, **and Feng** have finished editing **their** film.

NOTE   Revise awkward constructions caused by antecedents that are different genders.

AWKWARD   Either Ernest or Alice will play his guitar.
REVISED   Either Alice will play her guitar, or Ernest will play his.

Today it is acceptable to use the singular *they* to describe an unknown person. In addition, it is acceptable to use the pronoun *they* in a gender-neutral way to describe a known person who does not use gender-specific pronouns such as *he* or *she.*

5w   **When a singular and a plural antecedent are joined by *or* or *nor,* the pronoun usually agrees with the nearer antecedent.**

EXAMPLES   Neither the **puppies nor** our full-grown **dog** likes **its** new dishes.
Neither our full-grown **dog nor** the **puppies** like **their** new dishes.

Whenever possible, revise the sentence to avoid such an awkward construction.

EXAMPLE   The **puppies** don't like **their** new dishes, and our full-grown **dog** doesn't like **its** new dishes either.

EXERCISE 11   Using Pronouns That Agree with Antecedents

In the following sentences, fill in each blank with a pronoun that agrees with its antecedent.

EX.   All of the women completed _____*their*___ work.

1. Before the debate, Miguel reviewed _____ note cards.

2. How does the snake shed _____ skin?

3. Carl, Sara, and Reggie had _____ essays published in an online literary journal.

4. Does the film live up to _____ reputation?

5. Wendy identified the unclaimed gloves as _____ .

6. Will either Mom or Emily volunteer _____ time?

7. Robert practiced _____ German with the exchange student.

8. My friend Zoe has been performing Indian classical dance since _____ was six years old.

9. The photo essay speaks for _____ .

10. When I see Gerald and Patti, I'll tell _____ about the party.

11. Everyone who is going on the class trip needs to bring _____ deposit on Monday.

12. Neither John nor Adam is ready to give _____ report.

13. Contestants must submit _____ artwork before next Friday.

14. Dawn developed the advertising campaign _____ .

15. Neither Pedro nor Walter took _____ case to court.

16. Will scientists from several countries share _____ findings at the conference?

17. All of the spectators showed _____ appreciation by applauding and cheering.

18. Each of the actors wore _____ costume.

19. Is Ms. Gutiérrez visiting _____ niece in Arizona?

20. The geese are returning from _____ winter homes.

EXERCISE 12   Proofreading a Paragraph for Pronoun-Antecedent Agreement

In the paragraphs below, draw a line through the errors in pronoun-antecedent agreement. Write your corrections above the error. If a sentence does not contain an error, write *C*.

EX.   In the world of Impressionist painting, Mary Cassatt made ~~their~~ *her* work known.

[1] Like many other female painters, Mary Cassatt found himself surrounded by the works and ideas of men. [2] Neither the painters she studied nor the instructors who taught her were female. [3] However, what Cassatt learned on his own she applied to her paintings. [4] The pastel colors that Cassatt used characterize their best work. [5] After some Impressionist artists saw some of Cassatt's paintings at an 1874 exhibit, nearly everyone agreed that her work was among the best. [6] Certainly no one could truthfully claim that their work was better than Cassatt's.

[7] Edgar Degas suggested that Cassatt create a series of paintings, and she accepted her suggestion. [8] All of the paintings in the series had mothers and children as its subject. [9] Many critics think the series themselves is Cassatt's most important work. [10] Cassatt painted women and children in her everyday domestic lives with few traces of sentimentality. [11] Each subject seemed to have their own identity. [12] *The Bath* shows a mother washing their daughter's feet and is typical of Cassatt's affection for her subjects.

[13] The Impressionist painters allowed Cassatt to act as a sort of art dealer for his and her paintings. [14] Cassatt had wealthy friends and relatives in the United States who bought their paintings and those of other Impressionist artists. [15] Some American painters today are aware of Cassatt's influence on his work.

MODULE REVIEW

A. Proofreading Sentences for Subject-Verb and Pronoun-Antecedent Agreement

In each of the sentences below, draw a line though any errors in subject-verb agreement or pronoun-antecedent agreement. Then, on the line before the sentence, write your correction. If a sentence contains no errors, write *C*.

EX. ___*is*___ The jewelry that Inez makes ~~are~~ based on Navajo designs.

_____ 1. The average height for a sunflower are 10 feet.

_____ 2. Computer programmer and analyst is one of the jobs in which I am interested.

_____ 3. All of the teachers have her master's degrees.

_____ 4. A number of squirrels has made their home in that tree.

_____ 5. No one from the ballet company is rehearsing their parts.

_____ 6. Either David or Kyle will read their poem next.

_____ 7. Marta, as well as her parents, are joining us for dinner.

_____ 8. Some of the exhibit showcases Japanese textile arts.

_____ 9. The scissors is kept in a locked drawer.

_____ 10. Everyone is disagreeing about the concert schedule.

_____ 11. Both New York and New Jersey held its elections this year.

_____ 12. Neither Jupiter nor its moons is visible under these conditions.

_____ 13. The quartet are performing several Mozart compositions.

_____ 14. Designing computers requires specialized training.

_____ 15. Many in the community participates in a neighborhood watch program.

_____ 16. What Jen is doing to earn extra money are shoveling snow and chopping firewood.

_____ 17. The mare tended its foal.

_____ 18. Two-thirds of the vote assures a victory.

_____ 19. Neither of the undefeated teams expect to lose the game.

_____ 20. All of the reporters showed his or her credentials.

B. Proofreading a Paragraph for Errors in Subject-Verb and Pronoun-Antecedent Agreement

In the paragraph below, draw a line through any errors in subject-verb agreement or pronoun-antecedent agreement. Write your correction in the space above the incorrect word. If a sentence has no agreement errors, write *C*.

have
EX.   Many cultures ~~has~~ unique methods of decorating cloth.

[1] Batik is one of those methods that has existed for many years. [2] People in

Southeast Asia has used the batik method for thousands of years. [3] In batik dyeing,

wax is placed on cotton cloth to form a pattern. [4] The cloth under the wax receive no

dye. [5] When the cloth is dyed and the wax is removed, the pattern appear on the

cloth. [6] Brown, blue, and red is the traditional colors for batik. [7] Either

multicolored designs or a blended pattern are a variation of basic batik. [8] Wax from

the first design is boiled off. [9] Each new application of wax create a new pattern.

[10] In Java, many advancements was made in the art of batik. [11] The Javanese

artists' innovations allowed her to create highly detailed patterns. [12] In the 1700s, they was applying the wax with a specialized copper instrument. [13] The Javanese

were still using a woodblock process to apply the wax 100 years later. [14] Today,

modern machines duplicates the batik process. [15] However, authentic batik cloth are

still made by this centuries-old process.

MODULE 6: CORRECT PRONOUN USAGE
CASE OF PERSONAL PRONOUNS

6a   **Personal pronouns change form in different cases.**

A noun or pronoun in the ***nominative*** case is the subject of its sentence.

EXAMPLES   The **cashier** returned the change.

    He returned the change.

A noun or pronoun in the ***objective*** case is the direct or indirect object of a verb or preposition.

EXAMPLES   The store hired a new **cashier.**

    The store hired **him**.

A noun or pronoun in the ***possessive*** case shows ownership.

EXAMPLES   The **cashier's** uniform was blue.

    His uniform was blue.

Notice that the pronoun takes a different form in each case.

Within each case, the forms of personal pronouns indicate *number, person,* and *gender.* ***Number*** is the form a word takes to indicate whether it is *singular* or *plural.* ***Person*** is the form a word takes to indicate the one(s) speaking (*first person*), the one(s) spoken to (*second person*), or the one(s) spoken of or about (*third person*). ***Gender*** is the form a word takes to indicate whether it is *masculine, feminine,* or *neuter* (neither masculine nor feminine).

Notice also that only third-person singular pronouns indicate gender.

	PERSONAL PRONOUNS		
	Singular		
	Nominative Case	**Objective Case**	**Possessive Case**
First Person	I	me	my, mine
Second Person	you	you	your, yours
Third Person	he, she, it	him, her, it	his, her, hers, its
	Plural		
	Nominative Case	**Objective Case**	**Possessive Case**
First Person	we	us	our, ours
Second Person	you	you	your, yours
Third Person	they	them	their, theirs

NOTES   Some teachers prefer to use the term *adjective* to describe a possessive pronoun, such as *my* or *their*, that precedes a noun. Follow your teacher's directions in labeling possessive forms.

Today it is acceptable to use the pronoun *they* in a gender-neutral way to describe a known person who does not use gender-specific pronouns such as *he* or *she*. In addition, the singular *they* is used in informal speech to describe an unknown person and is also increasingly accepted in formal writing.

EXAMPLES   Someone puts the cans on the shelves and they also organize the fresh produce. (unknown person)
Mia just joined the environmental club. They are excited to help restore local habitats. (known person)

EXERCISE 1   Identifying Personal Pronouns and Their Cases

On the line before each sentence below, identify the case of the italicized pronoun by writing *N* for *nominative*, *O* for *objective*, or *P* for *possessive*.

EX.   _____P_____   *Our* class studied the Athabaskan people of the Yukon.

_____   1. Ms. Schultz, the social studies teacher, told *us* that many Native Americans live in Alaska.

_____   2. *I* was fascinated by the Athabaskans, many of whom live along the Yukon River.

_____   3. *Their* language is related to both Navajo and Apache.

_____   4. *My* friend Kele is Navajo.

_____   5. He also became interested in the Athabaskans when I told *him* about the similarity of the languages.

_____   6. To refer to the Athabaskans in their native language, you would call *them* Dene, which means "the people."

_____   7. Dene make their livings in traditional ways, by hunting and fishing, but *they* also work in nontraditional jobs, such as oil drilling.

_____   8. Many Dene try to live *their* lives in harmony with nature.

_____   9. Never in *my* life have I grown food or fished for my dinner.

_____   10. *We* could learn much from the Athabaskans, or Dene.

MODULE 6: CORRECT PRONOUN USAGE

THE NOMINATIVE CASE

6b   The subject of a verb is in the nominative case.

EXAMPLES   **She** feeds the fish. [*She* is the subject of *feeds*.]

Della and **I** wired the lights. [*Della and I* is the compound subject of *wired*.]

Ted told the manager that **we** had been working all day. [*Ted* is the subject of *told*, and *we* is the subject of *had been working*.]

A subject may be a compound with a pronoun appearing in combination with a noun or another pronoun. To help you choose the correct pronoun form in a compound subject, try each form as the subject of the verb.

EXAMPLE   (*She, Her*) and (*I, me*) took karate lessons.

Her and *me* took karate lessons. [incorrect use of objective case]

She and *I* took karate lessons. [correct use of nominative case]

ANSWER   **She** and **I** took karate lessons.

6c   A predicate nominative is in the nominative case.

A *predicate nominative* is a noun or pronoun that follows a linking verb and explains or identifies the subject of the sentence. A pronoun used as a predicate nominative always follows a form of the verb *be* or a verb phrase ending in *be* or *been*.

EXAMPLES   The goalie of the team is **she**. [*She* follows the linking verb *is* and identifies the subject *goalie*.]

The best speaker has been **he**. [*He* follows the linking verb *has been*.]

The last people in the theater were **he** and **I**. [*He* and *I* follow the linking verb *were* and identify the subject *people*.]

NOTE   In informal usage, expressions such as *It's me* and *That's her* are acceptable. Avoid them in more formal speaking situations, such as job interviews. In your written work, do not use them unless you are creating casual conversation in dialogue.

Like a subject, a predicate nominative may be compound.

EXAMPLES   The only students who participated were **Laura** and **Minnie**. [*Laura* and *Minnie* follow *were* and identify the subject *students*.]

The co-captains of the team are **he** and **I**. [*He* and *I* follow *are* and identify the subject *co-captains*.]

EXERCISE 2   Proofreading for the Correct Use of Pronouns in the Nominative Case

In the paragraph below, draw a line through each incorrect pronoun form. Write the correct pronoun in the space above the word. If a sentence contains no errors, write *C*.

EX.   If you and ~~me~~ want to become auto mechanics, we should study electronics and
     computers.

I (written above)

[1] Jake and me visited the science museum last Saturday. [2] Him and I wanted to see the exhibit on cars of the future. [3] It was he who suggested that we go because he knows of my interest in becoming a mechanic. [4] Jake introduced me to the exhibit's organizer, Ms. Cochran, and then Jake and her showed me some amazing things. [5] Them and I peeked under the hoods of electric cars and examined some computers that control engine functions and air conditioning and heating systems.

EXERCISE 3   Using Personal Pronouns as Subjects and as Predicate Nominatives

On the line before each sentence below, write a personal pronoun that can be substituted for the word or words in italics.

EX.   ___*he*___   Rafe and *Aaron* took a snorkeling class at the YMCA.

_____   1.   The instructors of the class were John Powers and *Emily Pratt,* two dive masters with lots of experience.

_____   2.   The best swimmers in the class were *Paulo and I.*

_____   3.   The most skilled divers in that YMCA class were Marsha and *Tyrone.*

_____   4.   We paired up into two-person teams, and Ms. Pratt said that one team would be *Mark* and I.

_____   5.   *Mark and I* practiced putting on our fins, clearing our snorkels, replacing our masks under water, and lifesaving techniques.

MODULE 6: CORRECT PRONOUN USAGE
THE OBJECTIVE CASE

6d   A direct object and an indirect object are in the objective case.

A ***direct object*** is a noun or pronoun that receives the action of the verb or shows the result of the action.

EXAMPLES   The phone call made **her** happy. [*Her* tells whom the phone call made happy.]
Someone asked **them** for free tickets. [*Them* tells whom someone asked.]

An ***indirect object*** is a noun or pronoun that tells *to whom* or *for whom* or *to what* or *for what* the action of the verb is done.

EXAMPLES   Christos told **us** an incredible story. [*Us* tells *to whom* Christos told an incredible story.]
Garth sent **him** an invitation to the party. [*Him* tells *to whom* Garth sent an invitation.]

6e   An object of a preposition is in the objective case.

A noun or pronoun used as an ***object of a preposition*** comes at the end of a phrase that begins with a preposition.

EXAMPLES   for **her**   under **them**   next to **you** and **us**

To choose the correct pronoun in a compound direct object, compound indirect object, or compound object of a preposition, try each form of the pronoun separately in a sentence.

EXAMPLE   Desi informed him and I.
Desi informed him is correct.
Desi informed I is incorrect.
ANSWER   Desi informed **him** and **me**.

EXAMPLE   We served him and they lunch.
We served him is correct.
We served they is incorrect.
ANSWER   We served **him** and **them** lunch.

EXAMPLE   The teachers gave apples to them and we.
The teachers gave apples to them is correct.
The teachers gave apples to we is incorrect.
ANSWER   The teachers gave apples to **them** and **us**.

EXERCISE 4   Using Correct Forms of Objective Case Pronouns

For each sentence below, underline the correct pronoun in parentheses.

EX.   Wanda told (*he, him*) about that exhibit.

1. The strong wind pushed Dwayne and (*I, me*) as we walked down the sidewalk.

2. In 15 minutes, Paco will join (*they, them*) on the stage for the musical's grand finale.

3. "Would you deliver these carnations and roses to (*he, him*) on your way home?" Kasia asked.

4. For three hours on Wednesday, I walked beside (*she, her*) in the neighborhood park.

5. Because Aaron is such a good friend, I wrote (*he, him*) a song about some of our experiences.

6. Parker told (*we, us*) all about his plans to go to junior college next September.

7. Rosa roasted the chilies and then served (*they, them*) to her guests.

8. I would like for my cousin Rashid and (*I, me*) to play a game of chess this afternoon.

9. I went with (*he, him*) to buy candles for the birthday cake.

10. Please tell (*we, us*) when the eclipse will begin.

11. I would like to invite (*he, him*) as well.

12. Give (*they, them*) information for the report.

13. You may borrow the books next to Dad and (*me, I*).

14. Ted reminded (*she, her*) that vacation would begin in two weeks.

15. I asked Tanya to help (*I, me*) pick out a bonsai tree.

16. Help Sam and (*she, her*) paint the fence.

17. My mother tutored Pedro and (*he, him*) in algebra.

18. Give (*we, us*) good directions to the museum.

19. Mr. Weitz showed (*they, them*) his handmade porcelain dolls.

20. "She crossed the finish line ahead of (*I, me*)," Brent said to the coach.

THE POSSESSIVE CASE

6f   The possessive pronouns *mine*, *yours*, *his*, *hers*, *its*, *ours*, and *theirs* are used in the same ways that the pronouns in the nominative and the objective cases are used.

SUBJECT	Your shoes and **mine** are getting muddy.
PREDICATE NOMINATIVE	That bracelet is **his**.
DIRECT OBJECT	Patty, fill **theirs** first.
INDIRECT OBJECT	Can't you give **ours** a try?
OBJECT OF PREPOSITION	Compare these sample answers to **yours**.

6g   The possessive pronouns *my*, *your*, *his*, *her*, *its*, *our*, and *their* are used as adjectives before nouns.

EXAMPLES   **My** dog has no fleas.

His pants need mending.

Have I told you **our** group is going to Toronto?

6h   A pronoun preceding a gerund is in the possessive case.

A *gerund* is a verb form that ends in -*ing* and functions as a noun. Since a gerund acts as a noun, the pronoun that comes before it must be in the possessive case in order to modify the gerund.

EXAMPLES   **His** swimming was incredibly smooth. [*His* modifies the gerund *swimming*. Whose swimming? *His* swimming.]

Their jogging was a regular lunchtime activity. [*Their* modifies the gerund *jogging*. Whose jogging? *Their* jogging.]

Do not confuse a gerund with a present participle, which is also a verb form that ends in -*ing*. A gerund acts as a noun; a present participle serves as an adjective. A pronoun that is modified by a present participle should not be in the possessive case.

EXAMPLE   We watched **them** riding in horse-drawn carriages. [*Them* is modified by the participial phrase *riding in horse-drawn carriages*.]

EXERCISE 5   Using Possessive Pronouns

Complete each of the sentences below with an appropriate possessive pronoun. Do not use the same pronoun twice.

EX.   After we won _____*our*_____ game, we shook hands.

1. It's _____ necklace. I bought it at the fair last year.

2. I gave the diary to Lisa because I thought it was _____.

3. Is that _____ mother I saw you with?

4. If it's _____ toy, then give it back to him.

5. My mother made borscht using _____ grandmother's recipe.

6. Since the sports car was parked in your driveway, I thought it was _____.

7. _____ cousins are coming to visit us from Karachi.

8. Jon noticed the bee because of _____ buzzing.

9. _____ writing an original play was Maria's idea.

10. No, it's not _____. I've never seen it before.

EXERCISE 6   Proofreading Sentences for Correct Use of Possessive Pronouns

In each of the sentences below, draw a line through each incorrect pronoun and write the correct pronoun in the space above it. If there are no errors in a sentence, write *C*.

her
EX.   Tina tugged at ~~hers~~ boots.

1. We saw them walking together to the corner.

2. He writing always deserves praise.

3. "Her salad and your are ready," the server said.

4. Them playing a duet was my favorite part of the show.

5. Our searching turned up some terrific props for the show.

SPECIAL PRONOUN PROBLEMS

6i **Pronouns used as appositives should be in the same case as the word they refer to.**

An *appositive* is a noun or pronoun used with another noun or pronoun to identify or explain it.

EXAMPLES   The two best spellers, **he** and **she**, will compete in the finals. [The pronouns are in the nominative case because they are in apposition with the subject *spellers*.]
The trophy was given to the entire team, **him**, **her**, and **me**. [The pronouns are in the objective case because they are in apposition with the object of the preposition *team*.]

6j **A pronoun following *than* or *as* in an elliptical construction is in the same case as it would be if the construction were completed.**

An *elliptical construction* is a clause from which words have been omitted.

ELLIPTICAL   Ella was much more effective before the audience **than she**.
COMPLETED   Ella was much more effective before the audience **than she was**.

ELLIPTICAL   The dripping faucet bothered her brother as much **as her**.
COMPLETED   The dripping faucet bothered her brother as much **as it bothered her**.

The pronoun form in an elliptical construction determines the meaning of the elliptical phrase or clause. Be sure to use the pronoun form that expresses the meaning you intend. Notice how the meaning of each of the following sentences depends on the pronoun form in the elliptical construction.

EXAMPLES   I have been Luanne's friend longer **than she**. [I have been Luanne's friend longer *than she has been Luanne's friend*.]
I have been Luanne's friend longer **than hers**. [I have been Luanne's friend longer *than I have been her friend*.]

6k **A pronoun ending in *-self* or *-selves* should not be used in place of a simple personal pronoun.**

INCORRECT   Jerome and myself rode to the gym.
CORRECT   Jerome and **I** rode to the gym.

INCORRECT   Eva and Nolan brought gifts for ourselves.
CORRECT   Eva and Nolan brought gifts for **us**.

EXERCISE 7   Selecting the Correct Pronouns

For each of the sentences below, underline the correct pronoun in parentheses.

EX.   He gave the extra tickets to Marc and (<u>me</u>, *myself*).

1. Alicia has been a gymnast longer than (*he, him*).

2. Ray, please give a set of chopsticks to Geraldo and (*she, her*).

3. Because we had lived in town the longest, Mia and (*I, me*) gave the tour to the visitors.

4. The coach gave the captains, (*she, her*) and me, certificates of appreciation for our hard work.

5. I don't know the Bova family as well as I know (*they, them*).

6. "Are you unhappy with (*myself, me*)?" the puppy seemed to ask, as it sat by the broken vase.

7. The scientists, both (*she, her*) and he, discovered the vaccine.

8. Avery and (*I, myself*) are trying to build a 3D printer.

9. Two employees, Jose and (*she, her*), will bring their children to the company picnic.

10. The best drummers in the band, you and (*she, her*), should enter the competition.

11. Zora gave Roberto and (*me, myself*) some fresh oranges she had received from her grandmother in Miami.

12. My sister is more outgoing than (*he, him*) most of the time.

13. Reggie wants to invite his best friends, (*they, them*) and you, to the outdoor concert this weekend.

14. My brother Sheldon told us how they, (*he, him*) and his friends, used to put on plays.

15. Do you like the Indian dish *saag paneer* as much as (*I, me*)?

16. "I am as dedicated as (*they, them*) when it comes to raising money for our library," the mayor said.

17. Those two people, he and (*she, her*), are the photographers for the yearbook.

18. That ladder is as tall as (*he, him*).

19. Will you give Charlotte and (*me, myself*) a ride home from basketball practice?

20. We helped the children, him and (*she, her*), mold clay into animals.

MODULE 6: CORRECT PRONOUN USAGE

WHO *AND* WHOM

Nominative		Objective		Possessive	
who	whoever	whom	whomever	whose	whosoever

6l The pronoun *who* is called an *interrogative pronoun* when it is used to form a question. When *who* is used to introduce a subordinate clause, it is called a *relative pronoun*.

(1) The form an interrogative pronoun takes depends on its use in a question.

Who is used as a subject or as a predicate nominative. *Whom* is used as an object of a verb or as an object of a preposition.

NOMINATIVE **Who** wants to make popcorn? [*Who* is the subject of the verb *wants*.]

OBJECTIVE With **whom** did you go to the movies? [*Whom* is the object of the preposition *with*.]

NOTES In spoken English, the use of *whom* is gradually disappearing. Today it is acceptable to begin a spoken question with *who* regardless of whether the nominative or the objective form is grammatically correct. In writing, though, it is still important to distinguish between *who* and *whom*.

The use of the possessive *whosoever* is rare. Most speakers and writers today find ways to express their ideas without using this word.

(2) The form a relative pronoun takes depends on its use in a subordinate clause.

To choose between *who* or *whom* in a subordinate clause, follow these steps.

Step 1: Find the subordinate clause.

Step 2: Decide how the relative pronoun is used in the clause—*subject, predicate nominative, direct object, indirect object*, or *object of a preposition*.

Step 3: Determine the case for this use of the relative pronoun.

Step 4: Select the correct case form of the relative pronoun.

EXAMPLE She is the person (*who, whom*) I told you about.

Step 1: The subordinate clause is (*who, whom*) *I told you about.*

Step 2: In this clause, the pronoun is the object of the preposition *about.*

Step 3: As an object of a preposition, the pronoun should be in the objective case.

Step 4: The objective form is *whom.*

ANSWER She is the person **whom** I told you about.

EXERCISE 8   Using *Who* and *Whom* Correctly

In the sentences below, underline the correct form of the pronoun in parentheses.

EX.   (*Who*, *Whom*) were you calling?

1. Nolan Ryan was a ballplayer (*who*, *whom*) I admired.

2. Dad will give an extra helping to (*whoever*, *whomever*) asks for one.

3. (*Who*, *Whom*) is responsible for this confusion?

4. Do you know (*who*, *whom*) the president of Mexico is?

5. To (*who*, *whom*) shall we write this thank-you note?

6. Ms. Groat, (*who*, *whom*) is a chemist, will talk about her recent discoveries.

7. After I visited Austria, I began to read avidly about Mozart, (*who*, *whom*) was born there.

8. The class elected me to write to a famous movie director, (*who*, *whom*) may visit our town soon.

9. Can you predict (*who*, *whom*) will win the speech tournament?

10. Was it Lionel (*who*, *whom*) the band director asked to perform?

11. The Spanish Club served flan to everyone (*who*, *whom*) had a ticket.

12. I'd really like to know (*who*, *whom*) the judges selected.

13. Wilson is the only student in the class (*who*, *whom*) completed both an essay and an art project.

14. The senator (*who*, *whom*) I sent a complaint to wrote back to explain her vote.

15. Olivia will gladly be partners with (*whoever*, *whomever*) is left.

16. The principal said, "We need someone on (*who*, *whom*) we can depend to keep this project going strong."

17. When jogging, I smile at (*whoever*, *whomever*) I pass.

18. All the jugglers asked, "(*Who*, *Whom*) dropped the torch?"

19. Hal can't decide (*who*, *whom*) to ask to the prom.

20. Did you tell anyone (*who*, *whom*) did it?

MODULE 6: CORRECT PRONOUN USAGE

MODULE REVIEW

A.   Proofreading Sentences for Correct Pronoun Forms

In each of the sentences below, draw a line through any incorrect pronoun forms. On the line before the sentence, write the correct form of the pronoun. If the sentence contains no errors, write *C*.

EX.   _him_   Did you send a postcard to he and Emilio?

_____   1.   For who are you ringing that bell, Kesi?

_____   2.   Clem and myself wrote a program to compute batting averages.

_____   3.   At the audition, Andrea was called back more often than me.

_____   4.   The winners, Latoya and me, received free concert tickets.

_____   5.   The most popular actor in Hollywood is probably him.

_____   6.   Jeb told Libby and we some fun places to visit in Arkansas.

_____   7.   Him and Bert are making a movie about basketball.

_____   8.   We ran into Cara and them at the shoe store in the city.

_____   9.   The man whom you saw on stage is the mayor's son.

_____   10.   I could never be as good a quarterback as him.

_____   11.   Lori and myself bought new snowshoes at the trading post.

_____   12.   The next performers, Mario and me, will do a stand-up comedy routine.

_____   13.   Marco and them will be on a float in the parade.

_____   14.   It could have been us who got caught in that storm!

_____   15.   The ferry ride delighted her and him.

B. Proofreading for Correct Pronoun Forms

Draw a line through the incorrect pronoun in each of the following sentences. Write the correct form above it. Some sentences may have more than one error.

EX.   Aldo and ~~myself~~ *I* wrote a play about talking house pets: a dog, two cats, and a parrot.

[1] Him acting isn't very good, but Aldo's writing is excellent. [2] He writes more quickly than me. [3] However, I am the one whom does all the editing. [4] Ms. Carson asked Aldo and I to show the finished script to the drama director and she. [5] We four, Ms. Carson, the director, Aldo, and me, met to discuss the script.

[6] "Ms. Carson and myself love the idea," said the drama director. [7] "For who did you write the play?"

[8] "I have a little brother in preschool," I answered, "and as we wrote, I kept the preschoolers in mind and thought that there would be no better audience than them."

[9] "Well, Ms. Carson liked the play as much as me," said the director, "and we think that we'll produce it in the spring."

[10] "But first," said Ms. Carson, "our playwrights, Aldo and yourself, need to make a few revisions."

7a   A pronoun should always refer clearly to its antecedent.

In the following examples, arrows point from the pronouns to their antecedents.

EXAMPLES   **Phoebe** closed **her** math **book** and put **it** away.

When the **bells** rang, we could hear **them** for miles.

If **Sonny** arrives, tell **him** the news.

(1) Avoid an *ambiguous reference*, which occurs when a pronoun can refer to either of two antecedents.

A simple way to correct some ambiguous references is to replace the pronoun with an appropriate noun.

AMBIGUOUS   Kurt sent Henry a copy of the picture he had drawn. [The antecedent of *he* is unclear.]

   CLEAR   Kurt sent **Henry** a copy of the picture **Henry** had drawn.

AMBIGUOUS   After the server brought my sister dessert, she asked her for her check. [The antecedents of *she* and *her* are not clear.]

   CLEAR   After the server brought dessert, my **sister** asked for **her** check.

   CLEAR   My **sister** asked for **her** check after the server had brought dessert.

(2) Avoid a *general reference*, which occurs when a pronoun refers to a general idea rather than to a specific word or group of words.

The pronouns commonly used in making general references are *it*, *this*, *that*, *which*, and *such*. To correct a general pronoun reference, either replace the pronoun with an appropriate noun or rephrase the sentence.

GENERAL   Luis made it home with the papers, which made us happy! [*Which* has no clear antecedent.]

   CLEAR   We were happy Luis made it home with the papers.

GENERAL   A siren rang out and the smell of smoke was in the air. This made the pedestrians leave the street. [*This* has no clear antecedent.]

   CLEAR   When they heard the siren ring out and noticed the smell of smoke, the pedestrians left the street.

EXERCISE 1 Revising Sentences to Correct Ambiguous and General Pronoun References

Rewrite each of the sentences below, correcting the ambiguous or general pronoun references. If a sentence is correct, write *C*. (There may be more than one correct way to revise a sentence.)

EX.   Pedro was arguing with Bill about a letter he had written.

Pedro and Bill were arguing about the letter Bill had written.

1. My cousin Freda writes poems and stories, which I think is quite admirable.

   _____

   _____

2. The candidate spoke clearly and to the point. That should show up his opponents.

   _____

   _____

3. Nika was surprised to find a parking ticket on her windshield.

   _____

4. There was a concert at the as the bowling tournament, and it caused confusion.

   _____

   _____

5. The corporal reported to the lieutenant that his patrol was missing.

   _____

6. I received a card from my brother and a book from my aunt, which made me happy.

   _____

   _____

7. Julio noticed that Kendrick was wearing his boots.

   _____

8. After Lauren's goat bumped into the fence, it kept right on going.

   _____

9. More than 200 people saw the play on opening night, which pleased the cast.

   _____

   _____

10. Isabel texted Abby while she was out.

   _____

MODULE 7: CLEAR REFERENCE

WEAK AND INDEFINITE REFERENCE

7b Avoid a *weak reference*, which occurs when a pronoun refers to an antecedent that has not been expressed.

To correct a weak pronoun reference, either replace the pronoun with an appropriate noun or give the pronoun a clear antecedent.

WEAK I attended the tennis tournament yesterday and saw Stefi win every one. [The antecedent of *one* is not expressed.]

CLEAR I attended the tennis tournament yesterday and saw Stefi win every match she played.

WEAK Every school likes enthusiastic students, so let's see some of it at the next student council meeting. [The antecedent of *it* is not expressed.]

CLEAR Every school likes enthusiastic students, so let's see some enthusiasm at the next student council meeting.

7c In formal writing, avoid the indefinite use of the pronouns *it*, *they*, and *you*.

An *indefinite reference* occurs when *you*, *it*, or *they* has no specific person or thing as its antecedent. To correct an indefinite reference, rephrase the sentence, eliminating the personal pronoun.

INDEFINITE In dance class, they teach us how to move our feet to the music. [*They* does not refer to any specific group of people.]

CLEAR In dance class, we learn how to move our feet to the music.

INDEFINITE In the advertisement it read, "Don't miss New England in the fall!" [*It* does not refer to any specific thing.]

CLEAR The advertisement read, "Don't miss New England in the fall!"

INDEFINITE You don't want to get caught napping in Ms. Finch's chemistry class. [*You* does not refer to any specific person.]

CLEAR None of us wants to get caught napping in Ms. Finch's chemistry class.

NOTE The indefinite use of *it* in familiar expressions such as *it is early*, *it is raining*, and *it seems* is acceptable.

EXERCISE 2   Revising Sentences to Correct Weak and Indefinite References

Rewrite each of the sentences below, correcting weak or indefinite references. If a sentence is correct, write *C*. (There may be more than one correct way to revise a sentence.)

EX.   You know scientists have discovered over 30,000 distinct species of fish?
Scientists have discovered over 30,000 distinct species of fish.

1. Katie enjoys using her new in-line skates and says it is her favorite sport.

_____

2. Duc is an excellent pianist, but he has never owned one.

_____

3. Some fish are saltwater fish. They require this to live.

_____

4. On the politics website, it discusses the presidential election.

_____

5. Ms. Wilson said that the museum was worth visiting, but it would take two hours.

_____

6. We missed the bus this morning. That is why we were late for school.

_____

7. Most people prefer truthful leaders, but some people think it is not important.

_____

8. Each December, our village strings colored lights on a twelve-foot fir tree.

_____

9. You need a sharp eye to find a well-camouflaged female bird.

_____

10. In many Japanese restaurants, they serve tea with each meal.

_____

11. Kari is very shy, but she doesn't show it when she's with our family.

_____

12. The spin class worked so hard that it made them breathless.

_____

13. In early motion pictures, they show the actors moving and walking very fast.

_____

14. My father is an art teacher at the high school, but I know nothing about it.

_____

15. On Thursday, Sara spent an hour at the library, but she didn't find any.

_____

MODULE REVIEW

A.   Revising Sentences to Correct Faulty Pronoun Reference

The sentences below contain ambiguous, general, weak, or indefinite references of pronouns. Revise the sentences below to correct each faulty pronoun reference.

EX.   On many of the radio stations in Nashville they play country music.
Many of the Nashville radio stations play country music.

1. Ben wondered if Sam knew what he looked like up on stage.

    _____

2. Write me a letter, and send it overnight, which will make me happy.

    _____

3. Blanche ran to the water's edge, dived in, and had a terrific one.

    _____

4. Have Sergio climb those trees, using the handholds. This will be good practice.

    _____

5. Dad congratulated me, and gave me a pat on the back, which made me feel good.

    _____

6. In the polls it showed the challenger cutting into the incumbent's popularity.

    _____

7. We saw the canoes coming our way and our friends waving. That made us wave back.

    _____

8. The dish crashed to the floor, and it broke.

    _____

9. My brother likes my cousin, even though he's always borrowing his jacket.

    _____

10. She spent an hour in line and the exhibit was crowded, which made her grumpy.

    _____

B. Revising Sentences by Correcting Faulty Pronoun Reference

Revise the following sentences to correct each ambiguous, general, weak, or indefinite reference. If a sentence is correct, write *C*.

EX. Mattie took a deep breath and started to sing, which made her guests cheer.
When Mattie took a deep breath and started to sing, her guests cheered.

1. In these statistics it indicates that inflation was lower last year.

_____

2. My brothers traveled to see the band live during their final appearance.

_____

3. Don't mix molasses with the honey because it might make the recipe too sweet.

_____

4. Pietro caught the pass, stepped toward the basket, and made it one-handed.

_____

5. Hetty kept singing that song over and over, which annoyed her sister.

_____

6. That clock, which is on the mantle, has needed fixing for the past three months.

_____

7. The team put on their uniforms and then went out to play it.

_____

8. In the country store, you knew there would always be bargains.

_____

9. Serena noticed Lorenzo was applauding enthusiastically, and that pleased her.

_____

10. When the egg landed on the sidewalk, it broke.

_____

REGULAR VERBS

8a   **Every verb has four basic parts called its *principal parts*: the *base form*, the *present participle*, the *past*, and the *past participle*. All other verb forms are derived from these principal parts.**

NOTE   When the present participle and the past participle forms are used as main verbs (simple predicates) in sentences, they always require helping verbs.

EXAMPLES   I **park** the car. [present of *park*]
I **am parking** the car. [present participle of *park*]
I **parked** the car. [past of *park*]
I **have parked** the car. [past participle of *park*]

8b   **A *regular verb* forms the past and past participle by adding *-d* or *-ed* to the present.**

Present	Present Participle	Past	Past Participle
drip	(is) dripping	dripped	(have) dripped
patch	(is) patching	patched	(have) patched
propose	(is) proposing	proposed	(have) proposed
report	(is) reporting	reported	(have) reported

When forming the past and past participle of regular verbs, don't make the common mistake of leaving off the *-d* or *-ed* ending. Pay particular attention to the forms of the verbs *ask*, *attack*, *drown*, *prejudice*, *risk*, *suppose*, and *use*.

INCORRECT   We use to have several huskies.
  CORRECT   We **used** to have several huskies.

NOTE   A few regular verbs have alternate past and past participle forms ending in *-t*. For example, the past form of *burn* is *burned* or *burnt*.

EXERCISE 1   Writing the Correct Forms of Regular Verbs

For each of the following sentences, decide what the correct form of the italicized verb should be. Write the correct verb form on the line before each sentence.

EX.   _____*repeated*_____   Frank *repeat* the definition to himself twice so that he would remember it.

_____ 1. The whole room was silent as Mary *play* her flute solo.

_____ 2. Manuel *burn* dinner because he was watching a television program about life in the United States.

_____ 3. For exercise, Claire *walk* to school every day, except when the weather was bad.

_____ 4. I am *watch* that bird carefully because it may be a rare species for this area.

_____ 5. The package I am *expect* contains travel information for my trip to Oaxaca, Mexico, including some useful information on Oaxaca's customs and culture.

_____ 6. The remarks by the witness have *prejudice* the jury against the defendant.

_____ 7. Since we moved to San Francisco, I have *celebrate* the Chinese New Year each year with Won and his family.

_____ 8. Carlotta's mother has *list* on this recipe card the ingredients for her famous salsa.

_____ 9. I am reading right now, but when I have *finish*, I will help you with your math.

_____ 10. The painting was of Wolf Chief, a leader of the Mandan Indians who *use* to occupy much of the northern Great Plains.

_____ 11. We *phone* every member to tell them the meeting was canceled.

_____ 12. While Ben is *pay* for his lunch, let's find a table and save him a seat.

_____ 13. Many firefighters have *risk* their lives to save people from burning homes.

_____ 14. Jack is *paint* a portrait of his mother for her birthday.

_____ 15. After 30 years of teaching social studies, Mrs. Polanski is *retire* next spring.

_____ 16. Did you know that the first toothbrush was *develop* in China hundreds of years ago?

_____ 17. I got nervous giving my speech, so I *imagine* the audience was not there.

_____ 18. Mr. Klein is *share* an answer key to each test so we can correct our mistakes.

_____ 19. Not knowing what his shadow was, my cat has *attack* it several times.

_____ 20. Jane *ask* a passerby for directions to the theater where the performance was being held.

IRREGULAR VERBS

8c An *irregular verb* forms the past and past participle in some other way than by adding *-d* or *-ed* to the present form.

Present	Present Participle	Past	Past Participle
hit	(is) hitting	hit	(have) hit
leave	(is) leaving	left	(have) left
ride	(is) riding	rode	(have) ridden
sing	(is) singing	sang	(have) sung

When forming the past and past participle of irregular verbs, avoid these common errors.

(1) Do not use the past form with a helping verb.

INCORRECT   Has Velma rode that hobbyhorse before?

CORRECT   **Has** Velma **ridden** that hobbyhorse before?

(2) Do not use the past participle form without a helping verb.

INCORRECT   I sung the national anthem at the game.

CORRECT   I **sang** the national anthem at the game.

(3) Do not add *-d*, *-ed*, or *-t* to the present form.

INCORRECT   The batter hitted the ball with a satisfying crack.

CORRECT   The batter **hit** the ball with a satisfying crack.

NOTE   If you are not sure about the principal parts of a verb, look in a dictionary. Entries for irregular verbs give the principal parts.

COMMON IRREGULAR VERBS			
Present	**Present Participle**	**Past**	**Past Participle**
be	(is) being	was, were	(have) been
become	(is) becoming	became	(have) become
begin	(is) beginning	began	(have) begun
bite	(is) biting	bit	(have) bitten *or* bit
blow	(is) blowing	blew	(have) blown
break	(is) breaking	broke	(have) broken

COMMON IRREGULAR VERBS

Present	Present Participle	Past	Past Participle
bring	(is) bringing	brought	(have) brought
build	(is) building	built	(have) built
burst	(is) bursting	burst	(have) burst
buy	(is) buying	bought	(have) bought
catch	(is) catching	caught	(have) caught
choose	(is) choosing	chose	(have) chosen
come	(is) coming	came	(have) come
cost	(is) costing	cost	(have) cost
do	(is) doing	did	(have) done
draw	(is) drawing	drew	(have) drawn
drink	(is) drinking	drank	(have) drunk
drive	(is) driving	drove	(have) driven
eat	(is) eating	ate	(have) eaten
fall	(is) falling	fell	(have) fallen
feel	(is) feeling	felt	(have) felt
find	(is) finding	found	(have) found
forget	(is) forgetting	forgot	(have) forgotten
freeze	(is) freezing	froze	(have) frozen
get	(is) getting	got	(have) gotten *or* got
give	(is) giving	gave	(have) given
go	(is) going	went	(have) gone
grow	(is) growing	grew	(have) grown
hold	(is) holding	held	(have) held
hurt	(is) hurting	hurt	(have) hurt
keep	(is) keeping	kept	(have) kept
know	(is) knowing	knew	(have) known
lead	(is) leading	led	(have) led
lend	(is) lending	lent	(have) lent
lose	(is) losing	lost	(have) lost
make	(is) making	made	(have) made
meet	(is) meeting	met	(have) met
put	(is) putting	put	(have) put
ride	(is) riding	rode	(have) ridden

COMMON IRREGULAR VERBS

Present	Present Participle	Past	Past Participle
ring	(is) ringing	rang	(have) rung
run	(is) running	ran	(have) run
say	(is) saying	said	(have) said
see	(is) seeing	saw	(have) seen
sell	(is) selling	sold	(have) sold
send	(is) sending	sent	(have) sent
show	(is) showing	showed	(have) shown
shrink	(is) shrinking	shrank *or* shrunk	(have) shrunk *or* (have) shrunken
sing	(is) singing	sang	(have) sung
sink	(is) sinking	sank *or* sunk	(have) sunk
speak	(is) speaking	spoke	(have) spoken
stand	(is) standing	stood	(have) stood
steal	(is) stealing	stole	(have) stolen
swim	(is) swimming	swam	(have) swum
swing	(is) swinging	swung	(have) swung
take	(is) taking	took	(have) taken
tell	(is) telling	told	(have) told
throw	(is) throwing	threw	(have) thrown
wear	(is) wearing	wore	(have) worn
win	(is) winning	won	(have) won
write	(is) writing	wrote	(have) written

EXERCISE 2   Writing Past and Past Participle Forms of Irregular Verbs

Complete the following sentences by writing the correct past or past participle form of the verb in italics on the line in each sentence.

EX.   Kim (*lend*) __*lent*__ me her art supplies for the weekend so that I could finish my project.

1. Ian has (*sing*) _____ a solo in the spring concert for the last four years.

2. My uncle Nikimo will take us ice fishing when the lake has (*freeze*) _____.

3. I have (*make*) _____ many new friends since I became a volunteer at the hospital.

4. We have (*buy*) _____ our fruits and vegetables at Mr. Coviello's farm stand for years.

5. The bags were so full of apples that they (*burst*) _____ at the seams.

6. I have (*forget*) _____ how to install the software, so I'll have to read the manual.

7. For the science fair, we decided on an idea, (*draw*) _____ sketches, then built our inventions.

8. Joe (*run*) _____ 10 miles every other day for a month to prepare for today's race.

9. We (*go*) _____ to the youth center on Saturdays until we moved.

10. The Berlin Wall was constructed in 1961 and (*stand*) _____ until 1989.

11. My ancestor (*build*) _____ our house in 1896.

12. Lynette (*come*) _____ with us to see the virtual reality exhibit.

13. She (*ring*) _____ the doorbell three times, but no one answered.

14. Mr. Bell has (*send*) _____ me a copy of a book by the poet Julia Alvarez to read during spring break.

15. I (*eat*) _____ so much at breakfast yesterday that I was still full at lunchtime.

EXERCISE 3   Proofreading a Paragraph for Past or Past Participle Forms of Verbs

In the paragraph below, draw a line through the incorrect past or past participle verbs. Write the correct form in the space above the error. Write *C* above any sentences without errors.

began

EX.   The Hmong women ~~begun~~ a new way to keep their culture alive through the textile art of *pa ndhau*, or story cloths.

[1] Traditionally, the Hmong have gave hand-stitched squares as wedding or birth gifts. [2] The purpose of these squares was to honor the spiritual beliefs of the people and to bring luck and prosperity. [3] The Hmong women who were confined to refugee camps in the 1970s taked a look at what was happening to them; they realized that in moving from one place to another their culture could easily disappear. [4] Without the ability to use cameras or writing to document their culture, they knowed that they could use their sewing skills for this purpose. [5] Hmong story cloths vividly tell the story of the Hmong people; the beautifully stitched cloths have became graphic accounts of the Hmong history and culture.

MODULE 8: CORRECT USE OF VERBS
LIE *AND* LAY

8d   The verb *lie* means "to rest," or "to stay, to recline," or "to remain in a certain state or position." *Lie* never takes an object. The verb *lay* means "to put (something) in a place." *Lay* usually takes an object.

PRINCIPAL PARTS OF *LIE* AND *LAY*			
Present	**Present Participle**	**Past**	**Past Participle**
lie (to rest)	(is) lying	lay	(have) lain
lay (to put)	(is) laying	laid	(have) laid

The following example shows how you can ask questions to determine which verb—*lie* or *lay*—should be used.

EXAMPLE   The baby (*lay, laid*) among the pillows on the sofa.

Question 1:   What do I want to say? Is the meaning "to be in a lying position," or is it "to put something down"?

The meaning is "to be in a lying position." Therefore, the verb should be *lie*.

Question 2:   What time does the verb express, and which principal part is used to show this time?

The verb expresses the past, and the sentence requires the past form. The past form of *lie* is *lay*.

ANSWER   The baby **lay** among the pillows on the sofa.

EXERCISE 4   Choosing the Correct Forms of *Lie* and *Lay*

Underline the correct form of *lie* or *lay* in parentheses in each of the following sentences.

EX.   Pam (*lay, laid*) her books down next to mine on the kitchen table.

1. Lusita is (*lying, laying*) on the sand, watching the waves and listening to the gulls.

2. They have (*lain, laid*) down their brushes and are taking a break from painting the house.

3. Libya (*lies, lays*) north of Niger and Chad in Africa.

4. Jules has (*lain, laid*) on the couch for three days, recuperating from the flu.

5. While Amir is (*lying, laying*) out the bases, the players are warming up.

6. Before she began her workout, she (*lay, laid*) down on the mat and stretched.

7. The children are (*lying, laying*) in the grass to count the leaves on that tree.

8. A commemorative stone honoring the German and Italian immigrant families who settled the town was (*lain, laid*) in front of the town hall.

9. I (*lay, laid*) my books on the counter and handed the librarian my card.

10. I was so exhausted last night that I fell asleep as soon as I (*laid, lay*) on the bed.

11. My dog (*lies, lays*) next to the dinner table even after we've finished eating.

12. The problem (*lay, laid*) in his negative attitude.

13. Mr. Nakai was shocked when we (*lay, laid*) our finished reports on his desk two days early.

14. After my uncle (*lay, laid*) on a waterbed, he wanted one for himself.

15. The treats Mrs. Lopez made are (*lying, laying*) on the table.

EXERCISE 5 Proofreading Sentences for the Correct Use of *Lie* and *Lay*

In the sentences below, draw a line through each incorrect form of *lie* and *lay*, and write the correct verb form on the line before each sentence. If a sentence is correct, write *C*.

EX. _____*lain*_____ The book had ~~laid~~ on the shelf for so long that it was covered with dust.

_____ 1. He will dive to get the coins that are laying at the bottom of the pool.

_____ 2. If you see Lin, tell her I am lying down to take a nap.

_____ 3. Joe lay the last brick and stood back to admire his new chimney.

_____ 4. Your skates are probably still laying on the bench at the rink where you left them.

_____ 5. For the last three nights, I have laid in bed, unable to fall asleep.

_____ 6. Benjamin Banneker was appointed by President Washington to help lie a plan for the city of Washington, DC.

_____ 7. The Bohemian Forest lays to the west of the Elbe River and the Baltic Sea.

_____ 8. In terrible pain, Bill has laid flat on his back for a week.

_____ 9. Rosita lay her quilt on the table and nervously waited for the judges' decision.

_____ 10. They had not seen the "Wet Paint" sign before they laid their bags on that bench.

MODULE 8: CORRECT USE OF VERBS

SIT *AND* SET *AND* RISE *AND* RAISE

8e The verb *sit* means "to rest in an upright, seated position." *Sit* almost never takes an object. The verb *set* means "to put (something) in a place." *Set* usually takes an object.

PRINCIPAL PARTS OF *SIT* AND *SET*			
Present	**Present Participle**	**Past**	**Past Participle**
sit (to rest)	(is) sitting	sat	(have) sat
set (to put)	(is) setting	set	(have) set

EXAMPLES   **Sit** on the bench.   **Set** your umbrella in the corner.
Who **sat** here last?   Jo **set** the tiny chair on the shelf.

8f The verb *rise* means "to go up" or "to get up." *Rise* rarely takes an object. The verb *raise* means "to cause (something) to rise" or "to lift up." *Raise* usually takes an object.

PRINCIPAL PARTS OF *RISE* AND *RAISE*			
Present	**Present Participle**	**Past**	**Past Participle**
rise (to get up)	(is) rising	rose	(have) risen
raise (to lift up)	(is) raising	raised	(have) raised

EXAMPLES   In a pink haze, the sun **rose** over Los Angeles.
Ticket prices **rise** every summer.
Raise the signal flag of a disabled vessel.
Has the electric company **raised** its rates again?

EXERCISE 6   Proofreading Sentences for Correct Use of *Sit* and *Set* and *Rise* and *Raise*

In the following sentences, draw a line through each incorrect form of *sit*, *set*, *rise*, and *raise*, and write the correct verb form on the line before each sentence. If a sentence is correct, write *C*.

EX. *raised*   Bill ~~rose~~ the flag while the band played the national anthem.

_____ 1. Thurgood Marshall set on the Supreme Court for 24 years.

_____ 2. The lawn hasn't been mowed in five weeks, and the grass has rose above my knees.

_____ 3. When the sun is shining and the temperature is raising, I like to head to the neighborhood pool.

_____ 4. Vanna is sitting out corn and squash as part of her display on local farm products.

_____ 5. You should wait to begin eating until the server has sat down each person's meal.

_____ 6. The morning sun is raising above the horizon.

_____ 7. Our town has risen a monument to commemorate local veterans.

_____ 8. Sometimes, I have set in the waiting room for an hour before I could see my dentist.

_____ 9. Rob rises early every July Fourth so that he can find a good spot for our family picnic and for watching the fireworks.

_____ 10. Sit that package on the table, and I'll open it when I get back from lunch.

_____ 11. We set in our seats and waited for Dr. Spitz to begin his lecture on the renowned anthropologist Margaret Mead.

_____ 12. The choir rose money to supplement their annual food-and-clothing drive.

_____ 13. If I rise the height of my chair, I can work more comfortably at my desk.

_____ 14. The book Mrs. Stern has sat on my desk is by sculptor Isamu Noguchi, who carved a sculpture garden from a mountain at the Jerusalem Museum.

_____ 15. The fans raised to their feet as the home team scored its first touchdown of the year.

_____ 16. Please sit your knife and fork down when you are speaking.

_____ 17. The price of movie tickets has raised again.

_____ 18. For three years, I have set behind Antonio in math class.

_____ 19. Owen raised his hand to ask a question about Luis W. Alvarez, who won the Nobel Prize for physics in 1968.

_____ 20. Every afternoon, I walk through the door, and my dog is setting there, waiting for me.

8g The *tense* of a verb indicates the time of the action or the state of being expressed by the verb.

(1) The *present tense* is used mainly to express an action or a state of being that is occurring now. The present tense is also used to show a customary or habitual action or state of being; to convey a general truth—something that is always true; and to summarize the plot or subject matter of a literary work (such use is called the *literary present*).

EXAMPLES   On Mondays, Marcelo **attends** a yoga class. [customary action]
The Red Sea **gets** larger every year. [general truth]
Goldilocks **eats** the bears' porridge. [literary present]

(2) The *past tense* is used to express an action or state of being that occurred in the past but does not continue into the present.

EXAMPLE   Last Monday, Marcelo **attended** a yoga class.

(3) The *future tense* is used to express an action or a state of being that will occur. The future tense is formed with *will* or *shall* and the verb's present form.

EXAMPLE   Next Monday, Marcelo **will attend** his next yoga class.

The future tense may also be expressed by using the present tense of *be* followed by either *going to* or *about to* and the present form of a verb or by using a word or phrase that expresses future time.

EXAMPLES   Soon, we **are going to plan** the clean-up weekend.
Mr. Davidson **is about to begin** his opening remarks.
Our canned food collection **begins tomorrow**.

(4) The *present perfect tense* is used mainly to express an action or a state of being that occurred at some indefinite time in the past or that began in the past and continues into the present. The present perfect tense always includes the helping verb *have* or *has.*

EXAMPLE   **Has** Marcelo ever **attended** an advanced yoga class?

(5) The *past perfect tense* is used mainly to express an action or a state of being that was completed in the past before some other past occurrence. The past perfect tense always includes the helping verb *had.*

EXAMPLE   Marcelo attended the class because we **had talked** to him about its health benefits.

(6) The *future perfect tense* is used to express an action or a state of being that will be completed in the future before some other future occurrence. The future perfect tense always includes *will have* or *shall have*.

EXAMPLE   When his yoga classes are over, Marcelo **will have become** much more flexible.

Each tense has an additional form called the ***progressive form***, which expresses continuing action or state of being. In each tense, the progressive form of a verb consists of the appropriate tense of *be* plus the verb's present participle. Some tenses also include one or more helping verbs.

EXAMPLES   **Are** we **hiking** together? [present progressive]
           Was Natalia **climbing** with you? [past progressive]

Form	Examples
Present Progressive	am, are, is attending
Past Progressive	was, were attending
Future Progressive	will (shall) be attending
Present Perfect Progressive	has been, have been attending
Past Perfect Progressive	had been attending
Future Perfect Progressive	will (shall) have been attending

EXERCISE 7   Identifying Verb Tense

For each of the following sentences, identify the tense of the italicized verb. On the line before each sentence, write *PR* for *present*, *PA* for *past*, *F* for *future*, *PRP* for *present perfect*, *PAP* for *past perfect*, or *FP* for *future perfect*.

EX.   _____PR_____   The Erie Canal *connects* the Hudson River to Lake Erie.

_____ 1. The governor of New York State *had decided* in 1800 to link the West to the Northeast.

_____ 2. In 1817, the New York legislature *voted* in support of the governor's idea.

_____ 3. Many Irish immigrants *worked* to dig the Erie Canal, which was originally four feet deep and 40 feet wide.

_____ 4. The State of New York *spent* many millions of dollars to construct the canal.

_____ 5. The canal has a system of locks, which *fill* or empty to raise or lower a boat to its next level.

_____ 6. Boats *had traveled* part of the Erie Canal in 1820, but it wasn't completed until 1825.

_____ 7. In the beginning, travel along the canal was not fast; mules *pulled* the boats along slowly.

_____ 8. Merchants and sightseers *have made* the long, slow journey.

_____ 9. During the first years of the canal's use, a ride *cost* only pennies a mile.

_____ 10. In the mid-1800s, the ease and speed of the railroad *replaced* difficult canal travel.

_____ 11. It is difficult to use the canal all year because it *will have frozen* by the end of winter.

_____ 12. Since it was first constructed, workers *have increased* the size of the Erie Canal to seven feet deep and 70 feet wide.

_____ 13. Over 3,000 miles of canals *connect* various bodies of water in North America.

_____ 14. Today, most travelers *rely* on airplanes for long distances and cars for shorter ones.

_____ 15. Some day we *will have* a new method of transportation, and we may consider cars and planes slow and difficult.

_____ 16. Of course, the Erie Canal *was used* primarily for moving goods on barges.

_____ 17. Railroads and the interstate highway system *have caused* a great decrease in canal use.

_____ 18. Trucks *have* also largely *replaced* the railroads.

_____ 19. *Will* a more efficient means for hauling large loads *have made* trucks obsolete in our lifetimes?

_____ 20. Devising truck fuels that *cause* less pollution may preserve the trucking industry.

EXERCISE 8   Using Different Tenses and Forms of Verbs in Sentences

In each of the following sentences, change the tense of the verb or the form of the verb according to the directions given after the sentence. Write your revised sentence on the line provided.

EX.   She played basketball in college. (Change to present progressive.)

She is playing basketball in college.

_____

1. Pamela has completed a five-hundred piece jigsaw puzzle. (Change to present perfect progressive.)

   _____

2. Jason is building a wooden bird feeder as a present for Mr. Petner. (Change to future.)

   _____

3. The jewelry set includes seed beads, wire, and directions. (Change to past.)

   _____

4. After a long bus ride from Phoenix, the reggae band arrived in town. (Change to future progressive.)

   _____

5. Peter Jacobson has been playing music on the harpsichord for five years. (Change to present perfect.)

   _____

6. The bank on Main Street has an ATM with a Braille keypad. (Change to future.)

   _____

7. The class talked about a special show featuring sea turtles at the museum. (Change to past perfect progressive.)

   _____

8. By the end of her trip to Germany, Eliza will travel to Berlin and several other cities. (Change to future perfect.)

   _____

9. I read about a small, powerful microscope for examining objects indoors and outdoors. (Change to past progressive.)

   _____

10. Los Angeles, California plans to hold the Summer Olympic Games in 2028. (Change to present progressive.)

   _____

MODULE 8: CORRECT USE OF VERBS

SPECIAL PROBLEMS IN THE USE OF TENSES

8h   **When describing events that occur at the same time, use verbs in the same tense.**

EXAMPLE   The leaves fall and the air **grows** cold.
The leaves fell and the air **grew** cold.

8i   **When describing events that occur at different times, use verbs in different tenses to show the order of events.**

EXAMPLE   At present I **own** a Ford; my old car **was** a Honda. [I have a Ford now, so *own* is in the present tense. I used to own but no longer have a Honda, so *was* is in the past tense.]

8j   **Avoid the use of *would have* in "if clauses" that express the earlier of two past actions. Use the past perfect tense.**

INCORRECT   If you would have called the museum first, you would have known their hours.

CORRECT   If you **had called** the museum first, you would have known their hours.

EXERCISE 9   Using Tenses Correctly

In each of the following sentences, draw a line through the incorrect verb form. Write the correct verb form on the line before each sentence.

EX.   _*flew*_   In 1927, Charles Lindbergh ~~flies~~ across the Atlantic in 33 hours, but now the same trip takes about six hours.

_____   1.   Today, people watch television regularly, but before 1925, television does not exist.

_____   2.   The first musical Mickey Mouse films are released in 1929, the same year Herbert Hoover was inaugurated.

_____   3.   In October, 1929, the stock market crashed and an international economic crisis begins.

_____   4.   Paavo Nurmi sets a world record for running the mile in 1923, then won four gold medals in the 1924 Olympics.

_____   5.   If New York would have scored two more runs in the 1926 World Series, they would have been champions.

_____ 6. Calvin Coolidge was elected in 1924 and serves for four years as president.

_____ 7. *The Great Gatsby* was published in 1925 and had become a famous book since then.

_____ 8. In the 1920s, a new refrigerator costs less than 90 dollars; today, a new refrigerator costs hundreds of dollars.

_____ 9. Duke Ellington releases his first record in 1926 but did not gain fame as a jazz musician until the early 1940s.

_____ 10. Argentinian Enrique Tiriboschi swam across the English Channel in 1923; then Gertrude Ederle had crossed the Channel in 1926.

_____ 11. If President Harding would not have died in 1923, he might have been impeached for the Teapot Dome Scandal later that year.

_____ 12. A. A. Milne writes *Winnie-the-Pooh* in 1926, and it is still enjoyed today.

_____ 13. Emanuel Lasker has been the world chess champion since 1894; but in 1921, José Raoul Capablanca, a Cuban, won the title.

_____ 14. People ride street cars often during the 1920s but have lost interest over the years.

_____ 15. If you would have lived in 1928, you could have paid less than seven hundred dollars for a new car.

_____ 16. Born in 1924, William Rehnquist was 48 years old when he first sits on the Supreme Court.

_____ 17. The Harlem Globetrotters is organized in 1927 and still plays around the world.

_____ 18. Juan de la Cierva developed the autogiro in 1923, but now the helicopter had replaced it for the most part.

_____ 19. William Butler Yeats wins the 1923 Nobel Prize for literature; he had been writing poetry for many years.

_____ 20. Construction of the Cascade Tunnel began in 1926 and had ended in 1929.

8k The *present infinitive* is used to express an action or a state of being that occurs after another action or state of being.

EXAMPLE   Pepita had wanted **to catch** the four o'clock bus. [The action expressed by *to catch* follows the action expressed by *had wanted*.]

8l The *present perfect infinitive* is used to express an action or a state of being that occurs before another action or state of being.

EXAMPLE   The women had expected **to have moved** to Santa Fe by now. [The state of being expressed by *to have moved* comes before the action expressed by *expected*.]

8m The *present participle* is used to express an action or a state of being that occurs at the same time as another action or state of being.

EXAMPLE   **Reading** the map, Mosi gave us a choice between two routes. [The action expressed by *Reading* occurs at the same time as the action expressed by *gave*.]

8n The *present perfect participle* is used to express an action or a state of being that comes before another action or state of being.

EXAMPLE   **Having finished** in good time, we took the rest of the afternoon off. [The action expressed by *Having finished* comes before the action expressed by *took*.]

EXERCISE 10   Correcting Verb Tense

Rewrite the incorrect verb forms in the following sentences, using the correct verb forms.

EX.   Recycling most containers, they felt they had contributed to a cleaner and healthier environment.
Having recycled

1. Arriving early, Daniel decided to walk around the yard before he went in.

   _____

2. I should have known better than to underestimate your ability to finish on time.

   _____

3. Explaining how she calms herself before a race, the athlete then paced.

   _____

4. Vincent saved for six months to have bought a guitar.

5. Hearing recorded bird sounds for 15 minutes, the robin finally attacked the speaker.

6. Having begun with a startling question, Anita captured the audience's interest.

7. Lea would like to buy a USB, but she didn't get to the store before it closed.

8. Having quietly closed the door, Roberta didn't know everyone was still up.

9. Tsai learned to have danced by watching dance instruction videos.

10. Losing my notebook with my homework assignments, I texted Wren.

11. Your brother must be talented for him to sing with the choir for four years.

12. I would give anything to be at my cousin's first concert last month.

13. Having compared the two kinds of bears, Vida explained how they are similar.

14. Keiko's mother was so nice to cook for us when we visited them last week.

15. In his autobiography, he claimed to be lost in the Amazon rain forest for 10 years.

MODULE 8: CORRECT USE OF VERBS
ACTIVE AND PASSIVE VOICE

Voice is the form a transitive verb takes to indicate whether the subject of the verb performs or receives the action. Reminder: A *transitive verb* is an action verb that takes an object.

8o   When the subject of a verb performs the action, the verb is in the *active voice*. When the subject receives the action, the verb is in the *passive voice*.

ACTIVE VOICE   We **threw** stones across the water. [*We* performed the action; *stones* is the direct object.]

PASSIVE VOICE   The stones **were thrown** across the water. [The subject, *stones*, received the action.]

A verb in the active voice often has an indirect object as well as a direct object. When such a verb is put into the passive voice, either object can become the subject. The other subject then serves as a complement called a *retained object*.

                     S   V   IO   DO

ACTIVE VOICE   Our teacher gave the class a tour of the new school.

PASSIVE VOICE   The class was given a tour of the new school (by our teacher). [The indirect object *class* becomes the subject, and the direct object *tour* becomes the retained object.]

PASSIVE VOICE   A tour of the new school was given the class (by our teacher). [The direct object *tour* becomes the subject, and the indirect object *class* becomes the retained object.]

8p   Use the passive voice sparingly.

(1)   Use the passive voice when you do not know who or what performed the action.

EXAMPLE   **Had** all the books on China **been checked** out of the library?

(2) Use the passive voice when you do not know or want to reveal who or what performed the action.

EXAMPLE   The only copy of my term paper **was destroyed** last night.

(3) Use the passive voice when you want to emphasize the receiver of the action rather than the performer.

EXAMPLE   **Was** Tina's favorite teddy bear **found** by her brother?

EXERCISE 11   Identifying Voice in Sentences

Identify the verbs in each of the following sentences as active or passive. Write *A* for *active* or *P* for *passive* on the line before each sentence.

EX. __*A*__   We read about some unusual injuries.

_____ 1. A worker in Beijing, China, was rushed to the hospital.

_____ 2. He suffered from severe pain in the area of the intestines.

_____ 3. The doctors had seen the problem two previous times in recent weeks.

_____ 4. In all cases, the patients had been afflicted with pain after playing with a plastic hoop.

_____ 5. Their intestines had been twisted by the repeated rotation of their hips.

_____ 6. The hoops, light plastic rings, are spun around a person's body by the movement of the person's hips.

_____ 7. The hoop-spinning fad spread throughout China in 1992.

_____ 8. Youths in the United States were introduced to the joys of hoop-spinning decades earlier.

_____ 9. To prevent further incidence of intestinal injuries, doctors in China cautioned patients against using the hoops right after eating.

_____ 10. Proper warm-up techniques were also advised.

EXERCISE 12   Revising Sentences in the Passive Voice

Rewrite each sentence below, using the active voice.

EX.   During World War I, a serious concussion was suffered by Bela Lugosi, the star of *Dracula*.
During World War I, Bela Lugosi, the star of <u>Dracula</u>, suffered a serious concussion.

1. An injured soldier was being saved by Lugosi;

   _____

2. During the rescue mission, Lugosi was hurled into the air by an explosion.

   _____

3. The concussion was caused by his head hitting a rock on the ground.

   _____

4. His acting career, which had been interrupted by the war, was resumed once he recovered.

   _____

5. Being typecast as a horror-movie actor was disappointing to Lugosi.

   _____

MOOD

Mood is the form a verb takes to indicate the attitude of the person using the verb. Verbs may be in one of three moods: the *indicative*, the *imperative*, or the *subjunctive*.

8q   The *indicative mood* expresses a fact, an opinion, or a question.

EXAMPLES   Liliuokalani **was** queen of the Hawaiian Islands.
Shana **believes** that her school is the best.
Does Yuen Hui **have** a sister?

8r   The *imperative mood* expresses a direct command or request.

EXAMPLES   **Bring** me the gauze and scissors quickly!
Please **adopt** one of the puppies.

8s   The *subjunctive mood* expresses a suggestion, a necessity, a condition contrary to fact, or a wish.

EXAMPLES   Mom suggested that Aunt Latoya **read** a poem.
If you **were** on a safari, would you use a different camera?

(1) The *present subjunctive* expresses a suggestion or a necessity.

EXAMPLES   The waiter recommended that Pedro **try** the cold soup.
It is essential that Camilla **find** a larger apartment.

(2) The *past subjunctive* expresses a wish or a condition contrary to fact.

EXAMPLES   If Ben Franklin **were** alive today, would he be a politician?
I wish I **were relaxing** in a hammock.

EXERCISE 13   Using Subjunctive Mood Correctly

Most of the following sentences contain errors in the use of the subjunctive mood. If a sentence is incorrect, write the correct form of the verb on the line before the sentence. If a sentence is correct, write C.

EX.   __*be*__   Anna recommended that Alexis is in charge of refreshments for the party.

_____   1.   If dogs are allowed on the beach, then I would bring my German shepherd.

_____   2.   Tedra wishes that Peter was more agreeable to making changes in the organization's constitution.

_____ 3. She slept for only 15 minutes, but when she opened her eyes, she felt as though it was the next day.

_____ 4. The bird squawked as if someone or something was about to disturb its nest.

_____ 5. Darihuu Undarmaa, a professional contortionist from Mongolia, twists her body as if it were made of rubber.

_____ 6. It is essential that Cory locks her bike on the bike rack in front of school.

_____ 7. The class has recommended that Tom and Pearl are class leaders.

_____ 8. Mr. Finkel has proposed that all members of the science club are tutors for students in lower grades.

_____ 9. I wish I wasn't so nervous about flying; it takes some of the fun out of traveling.

_____ 10. It is important that Karina mails this package to her brother in Finland by express mail.

_____ 11. We had had so much rain that it seemed as though the sun was never going to shine again.

_____ 12. Mom suggested that Winona considers other people's feelings before speaking out.

_____ 13. It is urgent that he be allowed to talk to the officer in charge.

_____ 14. If he was around when we arrived, he could have explained what he wanted us to do.

_____ 15. The people had demanded that a mayor is elected who would work for a cleaner, safer city environment.

_____ 16. Mo acts as if Hakim was his best friend, although they just met two days ago.

_____ 17. Falling down for the third time, Shari said, "I wish I was as good on in-line skates as Kimmy Navarro."

_____ 18. The sales clerk recommended that _Selected Poems_ by Rita Dove, this country's first African American Poet Laureate, be included on our reading list.

_____ 19. "I wish Coach was here to see this," Benny whispered as the crowd went wild.

_____ 20. If I was a movie star, I wouldn't worry about anything.

A.   Proofreading Sentences for Correct Verb Usage

Identify the errors in verb usage in each of the sentences below. Draw a line through each incorrect verb form, and write the correct form of the verb above it. Write *C* if a sentence contains no errors.

EX.   Cammie wishes that her brother ~~was~~ *were* coming home for Thanksgiving.

1. If we had paid attention, we would have knowed that the quiz was today.

2. "I wish that this photograph of the Grand Canyon were clearer," Dave said.

3. If I were Tony, I wouldn't have wrote about such a confusing topic.

4. Violetta regretted the angry words she said to her parents the night before.

5. I didn't know that your friend Sue Ellen and my friend Lynda were sisters.

6. When the actor playing Grandfather walks on stage, the other actor is setting on the sofa.

7. The teacher asked Boris and Yoko to raise and tell the class about their cooperative assignment for English.

8. Having graduated from Harvard in 1890, W.E.B. Du Bois gave a graduation speech about Confederate President Jefferson Davis.

9. By the time our food gets here, we will be sitting at this table for an hour.

10. Miss Marotta had wanted to set and read to us about Chief Passaconaway, but she ran out of time.

B.   Proofreading a Paragraph for Correct Verb Usage

Identify the errors in verb usage in the following paragraph. Draw a line through each incorrect verb form, and write the correct form of the verb above it. Be sure all verbs are in the active voice. Write *C* if a sentence contains no errors.

EX.   *watched*
Penguins have intrigued me since I ~~have watched~~ a special about them on television several years ago.

[1] Having lived in Antarctica, penguins face many challenges as they attempt to travel from place to place. [2] These flightless birds spent more than half of their lives in the water, and they swim like fish. [3] They use their feet and tails to have steered themselves in the water and their strong flippers to push themselves forward. [4] I wish I was as fast a swimmer as a penguin, which can go up to 15 miles an hour! [5] Emperor penguins are incredible divers and have been knowed to go down a thousand feet. [6] No other bird has ever dive that deep. [7] Sometimes a penguin acts as if it was a porpoise and propels itself up and out of the water. [8] This ability helps penguins to have escaped predators when they're being chased. [9] By the time a predator is ready to strike, the penguin will leap out of the water and onto the ice. [10] Have you ever seen a penguin walking quickly across an icy, snowy surface, and think it looked as if it were about to fall over? [11] On land, a penguin has taken short steps and sways from side to side. [12] Their sharp claws are used by them to grip the icy surface as they hop from one block of ice to another. [13] When it has been necessary for them to move extremely fast, penguins resort to a special method of movement. [14] Penguins appear comical and clumsy as they slide across slippery surfaces on their fat bellies. [15] This method of travel is called tobogganing, and it's how penguins get around when they have wanted to travel fast.

C. Writing a Postcard

While you are on vacation, you decide to send a postcard to your friend back home. Use the internet to make a list of parks, towns, and local attractions that will help you describe your trip. Use five past forms and five past participle forms of the irregular verbs in the chart in section 8c. Underline the verbs you use.

EX.

> *June 23, 2024*
>
> *Dear Ramona,*
>
> <u>*This has been the trip of a lifetime. New Mexico is amazing! We had driven for two hours yesterday when we finally arrived at the Carlsbad Caverns. What an incredible place that was! I took some great photographs. Today we headed southwest on Route 180, toward the Rio Grande.*</u>
>
> *Brenda*

_____

_____

_____

_____

_____

_____

_____

_____

_____

_____

_____

_____

_____

_____

_____

MODULE 9: CORRECT USE OF MODIFIERS

USES OF MODIFIERS

9a Use an adjective to modify the subject of a linking verb.

The most common linking verbs are the forms of *be*: *am*, *is*, *are*, *was*, *were*, *be*, *been*, and *being*. A linking verb is often followed by a ***predicate adjective***—a word that modifies the subject.

EXAMPLES   That exam question is **complicated.**
                        Tuesday will be **fair** and **sunny.**

9b Use an adverb to modify an action verb.

An action verb is often modified by an ***adverb***—a word that explains *how*, *when*, *where*, or *to what extent* the action is performed.

EXAMPLES   Miguel **cleverly** avoided hitting the dock.
                        In the end, those who worked **conscientiously** were rewarded.

Some verbs may be used as linking verbs or action verbs.

EXAMPLES   Greta **looked** serious. [*Looked* is a linking verb, followed by *serious*, an
                        adjective.]
                        Greta **looked** seriously at the lock. [*Looked* is an action verb, followed by
                        seriously, an adverb.]

To determine whether to use an adjective or an adverb, replace the verb with a form of the linking verb *seem*. If *seem* makes sense in the sentence, the original verb is being used as a linking verb. If *seem* is nonsensical in the sentence, the original verb is being used as an action verb. Once you have determined whether the verb is an action verb or a linking verb, apply rule 9a or 9b.

EXAMPLES   Greta looked serious. [Since *Greta seemed serious* makes sense, *looked* is
                        being used as a linking verb and calls for the adjective *serious*.]
                        Greta looked seriously at the lock. [Since *Greta seemed seriously at the lock*
                        is nonsensical, *looked* is being used as an action verb and calls for the
                        adverb *seriously*.]

EXERCISE 1   Selecting Modifiers to Complete Sentences

In each sentence, underline the correct modifier in parentheses.

   EX.   Joshua played the piano (*wonderful*, <u>*wonderfully*</u>).

1. She walked (*confident*, *confidently*) onstage.

2. Guido grew (*proud*, *proudly*) at hearing his name called.

3. They asked us to send the flowers (*prompt*, *promptly*) to 10 Richardson Avenue.

4. Roberta always speaks so (*sincere*, *sincerely*).

5. The snowfall yesterday was (*light*, *lightly*).

6. Mandy seemed (*curious*, *curiously*) about astronomy.

7. Thousands of people (*enthusiastic*, *enthusiastically*) voted today.

8. The tired pitcher walked (*grumpy*, *grumpily*) to the dugout.

9. Those cards and letters made her feel (*cheerful*, *cheerfully*).

10. We liked the film because it presented the subject (*realistic*, *realistically*).

11. Please reach into that basket and (*careful*, *carefully*) pull out the plates.

12. Vanya (*desperate*, *desperately*) waited for the messenger.

13. After receiving the call, Sam left the theater (*immediate*, *immediately*).

14. We gazed as the clouds moved (*brisk*, *briskly*) overhead.

15. Right before the storm, the horses were acting (*restless*, *restlessly*).

16. The audience laughed (*loud*, *loudly*) at the comedian's joke.

17. The new teacher seemed (*efficient*, *efficiently*).

18. Everyone in the class was working (*diligent*, *diligently*) on the project.

19. Is it necessary to shout so (*loud*, *loudly*)?

20. The first-time soloist (*nervous*, *nervously*) waited for her cue.

MODULE 9: CORRECT USE OF MODIFIERS

SIX TROUBLESOME MODIFIERS

Bad and *Badly*

9c **Bad is an adjective. Badly is an adverb. In standard English, only the adjective form should follow a sense verb, such as *feel*, *see*, *hear*, *taste*, or *smell*, or other linking verb.**

INCORRECT   Too much salt made the soup taste badly.

CORRECT   Too much salt made the soup taste **bad**.

NOTE   The expression *feel badly* has become acceptable in informal situations, but use *feel bad* in formal speaking and writing.

Good and *Well*

9d **Good is an adjective. Well may be used as an adjective or an adverb. Avoid using *good* to modify an action verb. Instead, use *well* as an adverb meaning "capably" or "satisfactorily."**

INCORRECT   Molly writes short stories good.

CORRECT   Molly writes short stories **well**.

INCORRECT   You did good to tell the truth.

CORRECT   You did **well** to tell the truth.

As an adjective, *well* means "in good health" or "satisfactory in appearance or condition."

EXAMPLES   I saw Bill and he looked **well**.
Last week, Rhonda had the flu, but she feels **well** now.
All's well that ends **well**.

Slow and *Slowly*

9e **Slow is an adjective. Slowly is an adverb. Although *slow* is also labeled an adverb in many dictionaries, this usage applies only to informal situations and colloquial expressions, such as *drive slow* and *go slow*.**

INFORMAL   Walk **slow** and wave.

FORMAL   Walk **slowly** and wave.

EXERCISE 2   Proofreading for Correct Modifiers

In each sentence, underline the correct modifier in parentheses.

EX.   I hope my little sister did not behave (*bad*, *badly*).

1. As the museum director advised us, we moved (*slow*, *slowly*) through the exhibits.
2. Sabrena was determined to show them she could play (*good*, *well*).
3. Avoid eating fish if it smells (*bad*, *badly*).
4. The once-fertile fields along the Nile have been (*bad*, *badly*) affected by the Aswan High Dam.
5. Jasper steered the boat pretty (*good*, *well*), considering the high winds.
6. "Remember to walk (*slow*, *slowly*) down the middle of the stage," the director explained.
7. "How (*good*, *well*) do you know him?" Martha asked.
8. That hot dog tasted so (*bad*, *badly*) that Jiro didn't eat another one for a month.
9. The (*good*, *well*) student turned in her essay on time.
10. The face of the Sphinx in Giza is crumbling (*slow*, *slowly*).

EXERCISE 3   Proofreading for Correct Modifiers

In each sentence, draw a line through the incorrect modifier and write the correct form on the line provided. If the sentence is correct, write *C*.

EX.   _____*well*_____ Two days after taking the doctor's advice, she felt good.

_____ 1. He would have done good if he'd practiced a little harder.

_____ 2. The bumps on this road are bad.

_____ 3. Some Easter Island statues are damaged bad.

_____ 4. The instruction manual said, "Breathe slow and count to three."

_____ 5. Considering all that the survivors had been through, they didn't look so badly.

_____ 6. How good do you know this subject?

_____ 7. My uncle told me I shouldn't feel too badly about what happened.

_____ 8. The Inca raised the alpaca for its fur, which feels well.

_____ 9. The chef recommended that we chew our food slow to savor the flavors.

_____ 10. You'll have to speak up when talking to our dog Mortimer because his hearing is bad.

COMPARISON OF MODIFIERS

9f *Comparison* **refers to the change in the form of an adjective or an adverb to show increasing or decreasing degrees in the quality that the modifier expresses.**

There are three degrees of comparison: *positive*, *comparative*, and *superlative*.

ADJECTIVES	tall	taller	tallest
	hopeful	more hopeful	most hopeful
	good	better	best

ADVERBS	soon	sooner	soonest
	urgently	less urgently	least urgently
	well	better	best

(1) Most one-syllable modifiers form the comparative and superlative degrees by adding *-er* and *-est*.

EXAMPLES	small	small**er**	small**est**
	near	near**er**	near**est**
	late	lat**er**	lat**est**

(2) Some two-syllable modifiers form the comparative and superlative degrees by adding *-er* or *-est*. Other two-syllable modifiers form the comparative and superlative degrees by using *more* and *most*.

EXAMPLES	healthy	healthier	healthiest
	simple	simpler	simplest
	gladly	more gladly	most gladly

NOTE   If you are not sure how a two-syllable modifier is compared, look in a dictionary.

(3) Modifiers of more than two syllables form the comparative and superlative degrees by using *more* and *most*.

| EXAMPLES | considerate | more considerate | most considerate |
| | reluctantly | more reluctantly | most reluctantly |

(4) To show a decrease in the qualities they express, all modifiers form the comparative and superlative degrees by using *less* and *least*.

EXAMPLES	full	less full	least full
	visible	less visible	least visible
	calmly	less calmly	least calmly
	thoroughly	less thoroughly	least thoroughly

(5) Some modifiers do not follow the regular methods of forming the comparative and superlative degrees.

EXAMPLES	good	better	best	well	better	best
	bad	worse	worst	many	more	most
	little	less	least	much	more	most

EXERCISE 4   Writing the Comparative and Superlative Forms of Modifiers

On the lines provided, write the comparative form and the superlative form of each modifier below. Use a dictionary to check any words you are not sure about.

EX.   near
nearer, nearest

1. thick

14. green

2. clearly

15. fully

3. thankful

16. precious

4. gray

17. successful

5. little

18. happy

6. silently

19. likely

7. rapid

20. warmly

8. elegant

21. bad

9. dramatically

22. ill

10. long

23. tiny

11. elaborate

24. completely

12. much

25. good

13. narrow

MODULE 9: CORRECT USE OF MODIFIERS

USES OF COMPARATIVE AND SUPERLATIVE FORMS

9g **Use the comparative degree when comparing two things. Use the superlative degree when comparing more than two things.**

COMPARATIVE — Yesterday we walked to the park, because it was **nearer** our house than the lake was. [comparison of two distances]

It was difficult to tell which joke was **more humorous**, Millie's or Juanita's. [comparison of two jokes]

SUPERLATIVE — Of the three trees in the park, that old oak is definitely the **largest**. [comparison of three trees]

Hui Chun was a big tennis fan and enjoyed **most** of the matches. [comparison of many matches]

NOTE — In informal situations, the superlative degree is sometimes used to emphasize the comparison of only two things. Avoid such use of the superlative degree in formal speaking and writing.

INFORMAL — Ethel didn't know which she liked least, cold mornings or humid nights.

FORMAL — Ethel didn't know which she liked **less**, cold mornings or humid nights.

The superlative degree is also used to compare two things in some idiomatic expressions.

EXAMPLE — Put your best foot forward.

9h **Include the word *other* or *else* when comparing one member of a group with the rest of the members.**

INCORRECT — The crew went to Switzerland to film the Matterhorn, which is more photogenic than any mountain in Europe. [The Matterhorn is one of the mountains in Europe; it cannot be more photogenic than itself.]

CORRECT — The crew went to Switzerland to film the Matterhorn, which is more photogenic than any **other** mountain in Europe.

INCORRECT — Phoebe, who is secretary of the senior class, has a bigger vinyl collection than anyone in the senior class. [Phoebe is in the senior class; she cannot have a bigger vinyl collection than herself.]

CORRECT — Phoebe has a bigger vinyl collection than anyone **else** in the senior class.

9i   Avoid double comparisons.

A *double comparison* is the result of using two comparative forms (usually *-er* and *more*) or two superlative forms (usually *-est* and *most*) to modify the same word.

INCORRECT	Nora picked out the wristwatch with the more smaller face.
CORRECT	Nora picked out the wristwatch with the **smaller** face.
INCORRECT	Often, the first climber to the top was the most strongest.
CORRECT	Often, the first climber to the top was the **strongest**.

EXERCISE 5   Using the Comparative and Superlative Forms of Modifiers

In each sentence below, draw a line through the incorrect modifier. Write the correct form of the modifier above it.

sooner
EX.   Do you think Yuri will get there ~~more sooner~~ than Lita?

1. Vincent studies harder than anyone in his chemistry class.

2. Which of the three books did you enjoy reading more?

3. Which is least able to withstand the cold, an alligator or a lizard?

4. Robin Williams was one of the better-known American comedians of his day.

5. My dog Bowser was the most calmest of us all during the storm.

6. I've heard that Hercules was supposed to be stronger than anyone in the world.

7. Cristina ran quick, quicker than Ryan, and quickest of all the students.

8. Apples and oranges are both sweet, but oranges are usually more juicier.

9. Suzette, Fredo, and Rick saw the exhibit; Fredo was the more interested.

10. Which of the 10 largest cities has the worse pollution?

11. Yori's eyesight is rather bad, but his right eye is the least bad.

12. The most effectively publicized of the two candidates will probably win.

13. He was sure Taylor Swift could sing that song better than anyone.

14. The first act was bad enough, but the second was more worser.

15. My best friend asked me which I liked most, *The Lord of the Rings* or *The Rings of Power*.

A. Using Modifiers Correctly

The sentences below contain errors in the use of modifiers. Underline each error, and write the correct form on the line before the sentence.

EX. ___*easier*___ We could never find directions <u>more easy</u> to follow than the ones in that manual.

_____ 1. Marty could run more quickly than any member of the team.

_____ 2. Our captain guided the ship steady toward the harbor.

_____ 3. Of all the singers who auditioned, Sondra was the more extraordinary.

_____ 4. Tai Kwong usually approaches his homework quite thoughtful.

_____ 5. When I came to a fork in the path, I chose the easiest way.

_____ 6. Rocky later admitted he didn't eat the food because it tasted so badly.

_____ 7. Neil's garden contains the lovelier flowers on the block.

_____ 8. Do you think people go to the grocery store more than anywhere?

_____ 9. On our way to Colorado, we saw the more wonderful scenery.

_____ 10. My friend Leti draws better pictures than anyone I know.

_____ 11. In geography class today, some students were arguing about which had the hottest climate, Uruguay or Paraguay.

_____ 12. The team would have played better, but the quarterback had a cold and felt badly that day.

_____ 13. Aunt Shakita likes table tennis and bowling but still thinks that board games are the more fun.

_____ 14. If you're just learning to dive, make sure you avoid the most deepest parts of the lake.

_____ 15. While following the suspect, the detective looked careful at everything around him.

B. Proofreading a Paragraph for Correct Use of Modifiers

In the paragraph below, draw a line through each incorrect modifier, and write the correct form above the line. If a sentence is correct, write *C*.

                                                                              greatest
EX.   Some people consider Alexander Pushkin to be Russia's ~~most greatest~~ poet.

[1] Pushkin's grandfather was Abram Hannibal, a transplanted African who became famouser in his own right as a soldier fighting for the Russian czars.

[2] Pushkin wrote during the early 1800s and is still wide read in his native country.

[3] Some Russians, if they must choose among Pushkin, Tolstoy, and Dostoyevsky, will say Pushkin is the better of the three. [4] He was short and had a flat nose and a roughly complexion. [5] Some people have said that you could tell he was a poet because of how bright his eyes shone. [6] Pushkin attended school, but afterward, he quick entered the foreign ministry. [7] His early poems, "Ode to Freedom" and "Noel," were not received too good by the czar. [8] Because he spoke bad about the government in these poems, Pushkin was exiled to a place far away from the center of political influence. [9] However, because he loved writing poetry more than anything he had ever done, Pushkin used the time there to create his epic, "Ruslan and Ludmila."

[10] Eventually, he was discharged from his government job and returned home.

[11] From that time on, he did nothing but what he was better at, which of course was writing poetry. [12] Of all his later works, "Boris Godonuv" and "Eugene Onegin" are the more popular. [13] Both poems became well known part because they were later made into operas. [14] Pushkin made it clear in his work that he felt individual rights were no least important than those of the state. [15] A man whose life was often as dramatically as his poetry, he died fighting a duel at the age of 38.

C. Writing Sentences Using the Comparative and Superlative Forms of Modifiers

Movies are one of the most popular and diverse forms of entertainment today. Choose two movies you've seen recently and think about details such as acting, costumes, characters, and effects. Then compare the movies using comparative or superlative forms of 10 modifiers, either from the list below or modifiers of your own. Underline the modifiers in your sentences.

funny	heartwarming	incredible	well	silly
clever	loud	intelligent	dazzling	bad
little	colorful	sad	death-defying	suspenseful
ridiculous	good	strong	charming	beautiful

MODULE 10: PLACEMENT OF MODIFIERS

MISPLACED MODIFIERS

A modifying phrase or clause that is placed too far from the word it sensibly modifies is called a *misplaced modifier*.

10a   Avoid using a misplaced modifier.

To correct a misplaced modifier, place the phrase or clause as close as possible to the word you intend it to modify.

MISPLACED   Filling the air with thick smoke, we watched the charcoal burn.
  CLEAR   We watched the charcoal burn, **filling the air with thick smoke**.

MISPLACED   Jovita bought a new TV for the family which never worked well.
  CLEAR   Jovita bought the family a new TV, **which never worked well**.

10b   Avoid placing a phrase or clause so that it seems to modify either of two words. Such a misplaced modifier is often called a *two-way*, or *squinting, modifier*.

MISPLACED   Tell Gwen between acts I would like to see her.
  CLEAR   **Between acts**, tell Gwen I would like to see her.
  CLEAR   Tell Gwen I would like to see her **between acts**.

EXERCISE 1   Revising Sentences by Correcting Misplaced Modifiers

Revise each of the following sentences by moving the misplaced phrase or clause as close as possible to the word it modifies. Write your revised sentences on the line provided.

  EX.   Plants are sold by florists that grow in the tropics.
    Plants that grow in the tropics are sold by florists.

1. Jen talked about the illness she had had on the way home from the
  hospital. _____

  _____

2. Digging a hole with his front paws, Finn saw your dog Spike. _____

  _____

3. My neighbor has a parakeet who writes children's books. _____

  _____

4. We watched the clouds drift by eating our picnic lunch. _____

_____

5. I remember during a hurricane in Florida I was involved in the recovery effort.

_____

_____

6. Please put this vase near the TV on the table. _____

_____

7. He made a loaf of bread for his family that has raisins in it. _____

_____

8. The teacher asked the two students after class to report to the office. _____

_____

9. Lori said at the end of summer we would go to Santa Fe. _____

_____

10. We found a veterinarian for my cat who specializes in skin diseases. _____

_____

11. Please tell the neighbor on Monday I need the firewood. _____

_____

12. Hidden under the table, I can see your shoes. _____

_____

13. They learned at the museum she was a tour guide. _____

_____

14. A woodchuck dug a hole in the garden that is unbelievably deep. _____

_____

15. We hired for my sister a tutor who needs extra help in math. _____

_____

MODULE 10: PLACEMENT OF MODIFIERS
DANGLING MODIFIERS

A modifying phrase or clause that does not sensibly modify any word or group of words in the sentence is called a *dangling modifier*.

10c   Avoid using a dangling modifier.

You may correct a dangling modifier in several ways.

(1) Add a word that the phrase or clause can sensibly modify.

(2) Add, change, or delete words in the phrase or clause so that your meaning is clear.

(3) Reword the sentence.

DANGLING	The car went off the road while trying to read the map.
CLEAR	The car went off the road **while I was trying to read the map**.
CLEAR	I drove the car off the road **while trying to read the map**.

DANGLING	Talking about the game, dinner was forgotten entirely.
CLEAR	**Talking about the game**, Claudia and Shane forgot dinner entirely.
CLEAR	**Because Claudia and Shane were talking about the game**, dinner was forgotten entirely.

NOTE   A few dangling modifiers have become standard idiomatic expressions.

EXAMPLES   **Generally speaking**, a state park is the place to choose if you want to stay somewhere peaceful.

To be perfectly frank, that writer's only good book was her first one.

EXERCISE 2   Revising Sentences by Eliminating Dangling Modifiers

On the lines provided, revise each sentence to eliminate the dangling modifier.

EX.   To win the championship, an undefeated season is necessary.

To win the championship, our team needs an undefeated season.

1. While fishing, these trout were caught. _____

_____

2. Flying out of Cuba, the coast of Florida could be seen. _____

_____

3. Performing beautifully, her reward was loud applause. _____

_____

4. Extremely talented, singing and dancing are her strengths. _____

_____

5. The movie version seemed dull after reading the book. _____

_____

6. Missing Tanya, sadness filled the office. _____

_____

7. To do well in school, hard work is often necessary. _____

_____

8. Looking for our friends, the concert began. _____

_____

9. My travel plans were made having read about Samoa. _____

_____

10. Watching the children play, the afternoon slipped by. _____

_____

11. When training for a race, sturdy shoes are helpful. _____

_____

12. To learn about current events, news updates should be read. _____

_____

13. While hiking in the mountains, a storm began suddenly. _____

_____

14. Telling jokes and funny stories, their laughter could be heard. _____

_____

15. Built of bricks, strength is guaranteed. _____

_____

MODULE 10: PLACEMENT OF MODIFIERS
MODULE REVIEW

A.   Revising Sentences by Correcting Misplaced Modifiers

On the lines provided, rewrite each sentence below to correct the misplaced and squinting modifiers.

EX.   Blowing in the wind, we saw the colorful fall leaves of the conservation property.
We saw the colorful fall leaves of the conservation property, blowing in the wind.

1. According to one superstition, breaking a mirror for seven years brings bad luck.

_____

_____

2. Gwen made a costume for her brother covered with stars and stripes. _____

_____

3. Please give the woman a program in the blue suit. _____

_____

4. Painted by Alicia, Roberto hung the picture above the sofa. _____

_____

5. The firefighters spoke about the need for courage at a school assembly. _____

_____

6. Paolo cheered when Claudio crossed the finish line, also an Italian bicycle racer.

_____

7. These vases will hold several flowers that are made of marble. _____

_____

8. He built a boat for his cousin made from recycled materials. _____

_____

9. Jordan bought shirts that show the band performing before the concert. _____

_____

10. I want to ask my sister when she finishes her work to have lunch with me. _____

_____

B.   Revising Sentences by Correcting Dangling Modifiers

Rewrite each sentence below, to correct the dangling modifiers.

EX.   Standing on the riverbank, a large snapping turtle was seen.
While Emma was standing on the riverbank, she saw a large snapping turtle.

1. While watching the movie, my brother came home.

2. Begun as an experiment, Joe is now a successful businessman.

3. Looking at old photographs, memories came back.

4. To find the meanings of words, a dictionary should be used.

5. Having chopped the vegetables, the meal was ready to serve.

6. Listening to Erik's description, vivid pictures came to mind.

7. Anxious to begin the play, the stage was filled with tension.

8. Taking another helping of salad, his plate was full.

9. His confidence became stronger, thinking about past victories.

10. My face turned bright red, forgetting the poem I had memorized.

MODULE 11: A GLOSSARY OF USAGE

ADAPT, ADOPT / BEING AS, BEING THAT

This module contains a *glossary,* or alphabetical list, of common problems in English usage. Many examples are labeled *standard* or *nonstandard.* **Standard English** is the most widely accepted form of English. It is used in *formal* situations, such as speeches and papers for school. It is also used in *informal* situations, such as conversations and everyday writing. **Nonstandard English** is language that does not follow the rules and guidelines of standard English.

adapt, adopt   *Adapt* means "to change or adjust something in order to make it fit or to make it suitable." *Adopt* means "to take something (someone) and make it one's own."

EXAMPLES   We **adapted** the old clothes to make our costumes.
The Percys have **adopted** three children.

all the farther, all the faster   These expressions are used informally in some parts of the United States. In formal situations, use *as far as* and *as fast as.*

NONSTANDARD   Ten miles was all the farther the group could walk.
STANDARD   Ten miles was **as far as** the group could walk.

allusion, illusion   An *allusion* is an indirect reference to something. An *illusion* is a mistaken idea or a misleading appearance.

EXAMPLES   Her speech contained **allusions** to the legends of King Arthur.
The door really was a window, a cleverly painted **illusion.**

alumni, alumnae   *Alumni* is the plural of *alumnus* (a male graduate). *Alumnae* is the plural of *alumna* (a female graduate). As a group, the graduates of a coeducational school are usually called *alumni,* and *alumni* or the informal *alums* are acceptable gender-neutral options.

EXAMPLES   Because he is an **alumnus** of that university, he supports the scholarship fund.
The two women are **alumnae** of the same college.
The **alumni** gather every five years for a reunion.

amount, number   Use *amount* to refer to a single word. Use *number* to refer to a plural word.

EXAMPLES   The **amount** of food at the feast was astonishing.
The **number** of donations this year has increased.

as, as if See **like, as, as if.**

at Avoid using *at* after a construction beginning with *where.*

NONSTANDARD   Where are the newspapers at?

STANDARD   **Where** are the newspapers?

being as, being that Avoid using these expressions. Use *because* or *since* instead.

NONSTANDARD   My grandmother walks every day being as walking is good exercise.

STANDARD   My grandmother walks every day **because** walking is good exercise.

EXERCISE 1   Identifying Standard Usage

For each sentence below, underline the correct word or expression in parentheses.

EX.   (*Being as, Because*) a storm is predicted, the parade has been cancelled.

1. When the paved road ended, Rob said, "I think that this is (*all the farther, as far as*) as we can go."

2. The glittering decorations created an (*allusion, illusion*) of a starry night.

3. A huge (*number, amount*) of rain fell, causing widespread flooding.

4. We saw an enormous (*number, amount*) of geese flying south today.

5. We couldn't find the stray kitten's owners, so we decided to (*adapt, adopt*) her.

6. For the second time that day, he could not remember where his glasses (*were, were at*).

7. Twenty-five miles an hour is (*all the faster, as fast as*) you can drive near the school.

8. The (*alumni, alumnae*), who were all members of the Men's Chorus, keep in touch through social media.

9. Nina has a large (*number, amount*) of foreign coins.

10. In her poems, Kyra made (*allusions, illusions*) to her childhood.

11. The music was (*adapted, adopted*) from a classical piece by Beethoven.

12. He was late (*because, being as*) the rain had closed the roads.

13. Where should we (*meet, meet at*)?

14. It was hard to believe that the magician's tricks were just (*illusions, allusions*).

15. (*Being that, Because*) Anna's grandparents live in Denmark, she does not see them often.

credible, creditable, credulous   *Credible* means "believable." *Creditable* means "praiseworthy." *Credulous* means "inclined to believe too readily."

EXAMPLES   The teacher agreed that their reasons for being late were **credible.**

He gave a **creditable** performance in *Hamlet.*

The **credulous** audience believed that the magician could bend spoons using her mental powers.

data   *Data* is the plural form of the Latin *datum. Data* is frequently used like a collective noun, with singular pronouns and verbs. However, in scientific usages, *data* is always used with plural nouns, verbs, and pronouns.

ACCEPTABLE   The new **data is** here, and **it seems** to be accurate. *(if nonscientific usage)*

ACCEPTABLE   The new **data are** here, and **they seem** to be accurate. *(if scientific usage)*

emigrate, immigrate   *Emigrate* means "to leave a country or region to settle elsewhere." *Immigrate* means "to come into a country or region to settle there."

EXAMPLES   A variety of reasons cause people to **emigrate** from their home countries.

My grandparents were among the Ellis Island **immigrants.**

famous, notorious   *Famous* means "widely known." *Notorious* means "widely but unfavorably known."

EXAMPLES   The speaker is **famous** for her work with visually impaired children.

One **notorious** figure from folklore is the evil queen.

illusion   See **allusion, illusion.**

imply, infer   *Imply* means "to suggest something indirectly." *Infer* means "to interpret" or "to get a certain meaning from a remark or action."

EXAMPLES   In her remarks, the judge **implied** that it had been a complicated case.

From her remarks, I **inferred** that she had made a difficult decision.

like, as, as if   *Like* is usually a preposition. In formal situations, do not use *like* for the conjunctions *as, as if,* or *as though* to introduce a subordinate clause. Instead, use *as* to introduce a subordinate clause; use *like* to introduce a prepositional phrase.

INFORMAL   It looks **like** it is going to rain.

FORMAL   It looks **as if** it is going to rain.

EXERCISE 2   Identifying Correct Usage

For each of the sentences below, underline the correct word in parentheses.

EX.   Lucas seemed like a (_credible_, _credulous_) witness when the lawyers cross-examined him.

1. "What do you think this data (_show_, _shows_)," I asked my friend at lunch.

2. The speaker (_implied_, _inferred_) that she hadn't understood the question.

3. I would like to be (_famous_, _notorious_) for my writing one day.

4. Emily's excuse for missing the party turned out to be (_credible_, _credulous_).

5. Many Vietnamese (_immigrants_, _emigrants_) have settled in this area.

6. In his article, the reporter revealed that the person selling stocks at low rates was a (_famous_, _notorious_) scammer.

7. Wars and revolutions have caused many people to (_emigrate_, _immigrate_) to neighboring countries.

8. To our delight, the experiment worked (_as_, _like_) we had hoped it would.

9. I (_implied_, _inferred_) from the hastily written text message that Yoshi was worried about being late.

10. No one was (_creditable_, _credulous_) enough to believe Tony when he said that the Martians had landed.

EXERCISE 3   Proofreading Sentences to Correct Usage Errors

For each sentence below, draw a line through the error in usage. Then write the correct usage in the space above each word. If a sentence is correct, write *C* above it.

emigrated
EX.   Noni's family ~~immigrated~~ from Italy during the war.

1. The musician gave a creditable performance last night.

2. We can't prove our point without credulous evidence.

3. Mrs. Ramirez is becoming notorious for her beautiful photographs of the mountains.

4. The newspaper article inferred that the mayor was on vacation at that time.

5. I cleaned my room just like I said I would.

nauseated, nauseous   *Nauseated* means "sick." *Nauseous* means "disgusting" or "sickening."

EXAMPLES   The doctor asked if I was feeling **nauseated.**
          The factory was ordered to stop emitting the **nauseous** fumes.

notorious   See **famous, notorious**.

number   See **amount, number**.

of   *Of* is a preposition. Do not use *of* in place of *have* after verbs such as *could, should, would, might, must*, and *ought [to]*. Also, do not use *had of* for *had*.

NONSTANDARD   I should of bought my tickets right away.
   STANDARD   I **should have** bought tickets right away.

off, off of   Do not use *off* or *off of* for *from*.

NONSTANDARD   I bought some apples off that stand by the farm.
   STANDARD   I bought some apples **from** that stand by the farm.

or, nor   Use *or* with *either*. Use *nor* with *neither*.

EXAMPLES   We need **either** red **or** green paint to finish the poster.
          Neither Andrea **nor** Morgan had the right answer.

persecute, prosecute   *Persecute* means "to attack or annoy someone constantly." *Prosecute* means "to bring legal action against someone for unlawful behavior."

EXAMPLES   They were **persecuted** for their beliefs.
          The district attorney arrested and **prosecuted** the suspect.

some, somewhat   In formal situations, avoid using *some* to mean "to some extent." Use *somewhat.*

INFORMAL   After the holiday, the workers' spirits improved **some.**
   FORMAL   After the holiday, the workers' spirits improved **somewhat.**

than, then   *Than* is a conjunction used in comparisons. *Then* is an adverb telling *when.*

EXAMPLES   Lillian is taller **than** both of her sisters.
          First we ate lunch; **then** we went to the show.

this here, that there   Avoid using *here* or *there* after *this* or *that*.

NONSTANDARD   This here map is hard to read.

STANDARD   **This** map is hard to read.

who, which, that   *Who* refers to persons only. *Which* refers to things only. *That* may refer to persons or things.

EXAMPLES   Marcia is the one **who** has the key to the gym.

The teacher loaned her the key, **which** is the only copy.

It's also the key **that** opens the storage room.

EXERCISE 4   Identifying Correct Usage

For each sentence below, underline the correct word or words in parentheses.

EX.   The photographer (*which*, <u>*who*</u>) took this photo has an eye for detail.

1. Myra should (*have*, *of*) told us she needed a ride to school.

2. Neither Carmen (*nor*, *or*) Jenna has seen that play yet.

3. We planned to try every ride at the carnival, but after a few rides I began to feel (*nauseous*, *nauseated*).

4. The heavy winds eased (*some*, *somewhat*) by morning.

5. You could (*of*, *have*) told me you had no free time.

6. Mika got some good advice (*from*, *off of*) the veterinarian about how to care for her new dog.

7. Have you ever seen a robot (*that*, *who*) plays chess?

8. Our new car certainly runs better (*than*, *then*) our old one did.

9. (*That*, *That there*) magazine article described last year's earthquake.

10. First choose your topic; (*than*, *then*) write an outline.

11. Because they felt they were being (*persecuted*, *prosecuted*) by several people on social media, the two executives filed a lawsuit.

12. A (*nauseated*, *nauseous*) smell rose from the trash cans.

13. The attorney did not have enough evidence to (*persecute*, *prosecute*).

14. We can use (*that*, *that there*) bouquet of flowers for a centerpiece.

15. Ramona wants to prepare either chimichangas (*or*, *nor*) enchiladas for the potluck dinner.

THE DOUBLE NEGATIVE

A *double negative* is a construction in which two or more negative words are used where one is enough.

NONSTANDARD	We did not meet no people on the trail.
STANDARD	We did **not** meet **any** people on the trail.
STANDARD	We met **no** people on the trail.

barely, hardly, scarcely   Do not use *barely, hardly,* or *scarcely* with another negative word.

NONSTANDARD	There wasn't scarcely any rain this summer.
STANDARD	There was **scarcely any** rain this summer.

the contraction *n't*   Do not use the contraction *n't,* meaning *not,* with another negative word.

NONSTANDARD	I couldn't find no change for the parking meter.
STANDARD	I could**n't** find **any** change for the parking meter.
STANDARD	I could find **no** change for the parking meter.

no, none, not, nothing   Do not use any of these negative words with another negative word.

NONSTANDARD	Amy said she didn't have no more batteries.
STANDARD	Amy said she did**n't** have **any** more batteries.
STANDARD	Amy said she had **no** more batteries.

NONSTANDARD	Although we didn't hear nothing, the dog sensed the stranger at the door.
STANDARD	Although we did**n't** hear **anything,** the dog sensed the stranger at the door.
STANDARD	Although we heard **nothing,** the dog sensed the stranger at the door.

EXERCISE 5   Identifying Correct Usage

In each of the following sentences, underline the correct word or words in parentheses.

EX.   Because of her allergies, Layla can't eat (<u>*any*</u>, *no*) dairy products.

1. We heard fire engines, but we couldn't see (*any, no*) smoke.

2. There are hardly (*no, any*) fish in the pond.

3. Now that she has a part-time job, Zina (*has, hasn't*) scarcely any time.

4. Before he moved to Canada, Peter hadn't (*ever, never*) seen snow.

5. They ordered nachos, but the server said there wasn't (*any, none*) left.

6. Our seats were so far from the stage that we (*could, couldn't*) barely hear the music.

7. They searched where the map said the treasure was buried, but they didn't find (*nothing, anything*).

8. I hadn't (*ever, never*) heard of that state park until Tanya told me about it.

9. Julian said he had not told (*no one, anyone*) about the secret entrance to the cave.

10. Because of the blizzard, there isn't (*any, no*) school today.

EXERCISE 6   Correcting Errors in Usage

In each sentence below, draw a line through the error in usage. Write the correct form above the error.

EX.   I have seen scarcely ~~no~~ *any* cardinals this year.

1. We couldn't wait no longer for the latecomers.

2. Mirette wanted to buy mangoes, but the store didn't have none.

3. Do not pay no attention to what your opponent says; instead, watch what he or she does.

4. I haven't never seen a tornado, but I'm not complaining!

5. Tena said that when they moved to the city, they couldn't hardly see any stars at night.

6. Don't never touch a live electrical wire.

7. Zuri tried to find the door, but in the dark she couldn't see nothing.

8. The salesperson says that there aren't no more copies of that book.

9. Leo could not barely wait to read the next chapter in the mystery novel.

10. Because of the landslide, we cannot use that route no more.

MODULE 11: A GLOSSARY OF USAGE

MODULE REVIEW

A.   Correcting Errors in Usage

In each of the following sentences, draw a line through the error in usage. Write the correct usage in the space above the word.

> *Because*
> EX.   ~~Being as~~ Akio knows Japanese, we asked him to help us translate the poem.

1. Professor Plissas often uses historical illusions in her lectures.

2. Where do most of your relatives live at?

3. Lani didn't have no idea the paper was due today.

4. Maya borrowed skates and a hockey stick off Lisette.

5. The polenta tastes like it needs some seasoning.

6. Did you know that this movie was adopted from a Broadway play?

7. The police warned the townspeople to be on the lookout for the famous con artist.

8. "Trespassers will be persecuted," the sign said.

9. Shing reads much faster then I do.

10. The senator's speech inferred that the problem would be solved soon.

11. Neither the television or the computer worked when the power failed.

12. We had not scarcely arrived when the performance began.

13. That there building has been vacant for three years.

14. Cheryl feels like she needs warmer clothes.

15. The detective which solved the mystery was promoted.

16. According to reviews, her performance as Juliet is credulous.

17. Every year a group of male *alumnus*, sponsor a rally before the big game.

18. If I had known that the stores were closing early, I would of done my shopping yesterday.

19. After Gloria took the medicine, her headache eased some.

20. Anoki likes roller coaster rides, although they sometimes make him feel nauseous.

21. When we came to the fork in the trail, Michael said, "This is all the farther I can go."

22. I couldn't find nothing to read while I waited for the plane to arrive.

23. Have you checked to make sure that all the information is credulous?

24. When the car's engine overheated, we got some help off of the mechanic.

25. The amount of laptops in our school has doubled.

B.   Proofreading a Paragraph for Errors in Usage

In the paragraph below, draw a line through the errors in usage. Write the correct usage in the space above the word. If a sentence is correct, write *C* above it.

immigrated
EX.   Sook ~~emigrated~~ to the United States when she was eight years old.

[1] Her parents left their country because of political prosecution by the dictatorship in power. [2] In a dictatorship, the political power is either in the hands of one person nor in the hands of just a few people. [3] Under this type of government, people feel as if they have few rights. [4] Life must of been quite difficult for Sook and her family before they emigrated. [5] From what Sook has told me, I've implied that her family is very happy with their new life in this country.

C.   Writing a Newspaper Article

A well-known scientist who graduated from your school is making a return visit to unveil a new invention. No one knows exactly what it is. The scientist, who moved from Panama to the United States when she was quite young, has said only that the invention will greatly change daily life for the average person. You have been chosen to meet the scientist and to get a sneak preview of the product that she will unveil to the public later in the day. Your assignment is to write about your meeting for a local newspaper. The editor wants a description of the invention, along with some background information on the scientist. Write a brief article using at least ten of the following words correctly.

from	famous	nothing	amount
illusion	somewhat	adapt	number
emigrant	that	any	as fast as
either . . . or	as if	credulous	alumna
could have	then	creditable	alumni
prosecute	who	imply	data

EX. *adapt*

This invention is surprising in its complexity because it was adapted from a simple tool.

_____

_____

_____

_____

_____

_____

_____

_____

_____

_____

_____

_____

_____

_____

_____

_____

MODULE 12: CAPITAL LETTERS

PLACES AND PEOPLE

12a   Capitalize geographical names.

Type of Name	Examples
towns, cities	Rockport, San Juan, Tokyo, Bakersfield, Milan
counties, states	Riverside County, Essex County, North Carolina
countries	Taiwan, Bolivia, Saudi Arabia, Holland, Russia
islands	Tonga Islands, Anguilla, the Cyclades, St. Thomas
bodies of water	Lake Huron, Hudson River, Atlantic Ocean
forests, parks	Muir Woods, National Park, Lincoln Park, Yosemite
streets, highways	Madison Avenue, U.S. Route 66, Interstate 80
mountains	the Sierra Nevada, Mount Fuji, the Catskills
continents	Antarctica, Australia, Europe, North America
regions	the Northwest, the East, East Africa, Southeast Asia
divisions of the world	Arctic Circle, North Pole, Tropic of Capricorn

NOTE   Do not capitalize words such as *east, west, north*, or *south* when they indicate direction.

EXAMPLE   Maggie's poem was about the hills **n**orth of Boston.

NOTE   Do not capitalize the second part of a hyphenated street number.

EXAMPLE   West Forty-Second Street

12b   Capitalize the names of persons.

EXAMPLES   Mr. Starbuck, Ms. Hiro, Sasha, Jeannette Rankin, Raoul

Some names contain more than one capital letter. Usage varies in the capitalization of *van, von, du, de la*, and other parts of many multiword names. Always verify the spelling of a name with the person, or check the name in a reference source.

EXAMPLES   Mcknight   von Rosenvinge   de la Scale
            McKnight   Von Rosenvinge   De La Scale

EXERCISE 1   Correcting Errors in Capitalization

For each sentence below, correct the errors in capitalization by drawing a line through each error and writing the correct form in the space above it.

                                B   *S*

EX.   Toni Ramírez lives on ~~b~~each ~~s~~treet.

1. The irish sea lies between ireland and england.

2. According to an online encyclopedia, mount kilimanjaro is over nineteen thousand feet high.

3. The cities of Vienna, budapest, and Belgrade lie on the danube river.

4. The dead sea is very salty.

5. The fifth largest island in the world is baffin island.

6. Have you visited mesa verde national park in colorado?

7. The country of portugal is in the southern part of Europe.

8. The research team will be traveling through the arctic circle.

9. The largest county by population in the United States is los angeles county.

10. The directions say to turn north on langley road.

EXERCISE 2   Proofreading Sentences for Correct Capitalization

In the sentences below, correct the errors in capitalization by drawing a line through each error and writing the correct form in the space above it. If a sentence is correct, write *C* above it.

                   S   *I*   *B*

EX.   Ms. ~~s~~ilva drove down ~~i~~nterstate 93 to ~~b~~oston.

1. Writer kurt vonnegut was born in indianapolis, indiana.

2. Gretchen has an apartment on fifty-eighth street.

3. California's mount whitney is almost fifteen thousand feet high.

4. The cruise ship moved slowly through the persian gulf.

5. Is big bend national park in texas or alabama?

6. Hartford, albany, and providence are small cities in the northeast.

7. The colorado river empties into the gulf of california.

8. Enormous evergreen trees grow in sequoia national park.

9. The Southwest is known for its deserts and its big blue skies.

10. Thailand, vietnam, and laos are all in southeast asia.

SCHOOL SUBJECTS, FIRST WORDS, PROPER ADJECTIVES

12c   Do *not* capitalize the names of school subjects, except for names of languages and official course names.

EXAMPLES   geography   biology   orchestra   government
English   French   Algebra II   Science III

12d   Capitalize the first word in every sentence.

EXAMPLE   **T**he famous scientist, Ms. Chien-Shiung Wu, is our neighbor.

The first word of a sentence that is a direct quotation is capitalized even if the quotation begins within a sentence.

EXAMPLE   **T**ara said, "**S**ome of these Irish songs are really beautiful."

Traditionally, the first word in a line of poetry is capitalized, though many poets choose not to follow this rule.

The pronoun *I* and the interjection *O* are capitalized whether or not they are the first words of sentences. The common interjection *oh* is capitalized only when it begins a sentence or is part of a title.

EXAMPLES   "When can **I** schedule this work?" asked the dentist.
The folk song began, "**O**h, sing me a song of the seafaring life."

12e   Capitalize proper nouns and proper adjectives.

A *common noun* names any one of a group of people, places, or things. A *proper noun* names a particular person, place, or thing. A *proper adjective* is formed from a proper noun.

Proper Nouns	Proper Adjectives
Rome	Roman toga
William Shakespeare	Shakespearean drama
Haiti	Haitian art

NOTE   Proper nouns and proper adjectives may lose their capitals after many years of use.

EXAMPLES   watt   boycott   puritan

EXERCISE 3   Using Capital Letters Correctly

For each sentence below, correct the errors in capitalization by drawing a line through each error and writing the correct form in the space above it.

$$I$$

EX.   Kimberly said, "i̸/just love writing these verses!"

1. Nico taught us some lovely brazilian folk songs.

2. The team song began, "o victory, sweet victory."

3. Will you be taking geometry or algebra I this year?

4. One day hector will be a famous shakespearean actor.

5. Pauline asked, "just how tall is an alaskan brown bear?"

6. Marieke wrote a paper about the Aztecs for her Social Studies class.

7. the balalaika is a russian instrument that is like a mandolin.

8. This lamp takes three 100-Watt bulbs.

9. We needed furniture for the set of our play, so i rented some from a local

   antique store.

10. We learned some italian art songs in our music class.

11. oh, what a perfect day for a swim.

12. My sister Jasmine is studying ukrainian in college.

13. "I have studied latin, but I still can't speak it," said Mr. Robb.

14. The first sentence of julia's story was "at sixteen I learned to speak in

   confidences."

15. "Would you like some belgian waffles or some swedish meatballs?" asked

   the server.

16. In english class we studied the poetry of Countee Cullen.

17. What do you know about roman holidays?

18. Adrian said, "have you met my girlfriend, Pandora?"

19. In the mexican restaurant, soft guitar music played in the background.

20. have you ever been to Hawaii?

MODULE 12: CAPITAL LETTERS

GROUPS, ORGANIZATIONS, AND RELIGIONS

12f Capitalize the names of teams, organizations, businesses, institutions, buildings, and government bodies.

Type of Name	Examples
teams	Chicago Sky Charlotte Hornets
organizations	Habitat for Humanity Meals on Wheels
businesses	Riggs National Bank Seaside Cycle
institutions	Yale University Smithsonian Institution
buildings	the Alamo Empire State Building
government bodies	Library of Congress Cherokee Nation

NOTE The names of organizations, business, and government bodies are often abbreviated as a series of capital letters. If you are not sure whether to use periods with the abbreviations, look in a dictionary.

EXAMPLE   Federal Communications Commission   **FCC**

12g Capitalize the names of specific nationalities, races, and peoples.

EXAMPLES   Arab, Portuguese, Latin, American, Caucasian, Asian, Highlander, Iroquois, Shawnee

NOTE *Black* may be capitalized when referring to people, but *white* should be lowercase.

EXAMPLE   Black and white soldiers were usually kept apart during World War I.

12h Capitalize the names of religions and their followers, holy days, sacred writings, and specific deities.

EXAMPLES   Catholicism, Judaism, Muslim, Rosh Hashana, Easter, Koran, Bhagavad-Gita, Allah, Christ, Shiva, Buddha

NOTE When referring to gods in general, or when using the word *god* or *goddess* descriptively, use lowercase.

EXAMPLE   One of the most important Aztec gods was Tezcatlipoca.

EXERCISE 4   Identifying Correct Capitalization

Write the letter *C* on the line before each phrase that is capitalized correctly.

EX. _____   a. denver broncos

    _*C*_   b. Denver Broncos

_____ 1. a. Japanese American   _____ 6. a. Southwest Airlines

          b. japanese american   b. Southwest airlines

_____ 2. a. House of Representatives   _____ 7. a. Colorado state university

          b. House of representatives   b. Colorado State University

_____ 3. a. Washington Spirit   _____ 8. a. attending high school

          b. Washington spirit   b. attending High School

_____ 4. a. U. S. Coast Guard   _____ 9. a. the Old Testament

          b. U. S. coast guard   b. the old testament

_____ 5. a. buddhism   _____ 10. a. muslim scholars

          b. Buddhism   b. Muslim scholars

EXERCISE 5   Proofreading Sentences for Correct Capitalization

For each sentence below, correct the errors in capitalization by drawing a line through each error and writing the correct form above it. If a sentence is correct, write *C* above it.

                                      A

EX.   There are over three hundred thousand amish in the United States.

1. Devin is a troop leader for the boy scouts of america.

2. My sister Gianna now works for the bureau of the census.

3. Jada joined the Peace Corps to work in a developing nation.

4. The debate was sponsored by the league of women voters.

5. Do you think LeBron James or Michael Jordan is the best nba player of all time?

6. We bought some magnolias and forget-me-nots at silva brothers florists.

7. Does Rico really play tuba with the new york philharmonic?

8. Sydney took us to an authentic Sicilian restaurant called leonardo's.

9. When we were in Chicago, we visited the willis tower.

10. Who founded the hudson's bay company?

REVIEW EXERCISE

A. Identifying Correct Use of Capitalization

For each item below, write the letter of the correct form (a or b) on the line provided.

EX. ___*a*___   a. Colorado River

b. Colorado river

_____ 1. a. travel east on highway 8

_____   b. travel east on Highway 8

_____ 2. a. taking Math and English

_____   b. taking math and English

_____ 3. a. He said, "Please wait!"

_____   b. He said, "please wait!"

_____ 4. a. eating Korean Food

_____   b. eating Korean food

_____ 5. a. Oh, I wish I could go!

_____   b. oh, I wish I could go!

_____ 6. a. attending Westridge high school

_____   b. attending Westridge High School

_____ 7. a. living on East Twenty-third Street

_____   b. living on East Twenty-Third Street

_____ 8. a. buy it at Travel Bags to Go

_____   b. buy it at Travel Bags to go

_____ 9. a. reading about the Iroquois confederation

_____   b. reading about the Iroquois Confederation

_____ 10. a. coach of the Chicago Sky

_____   b. coach of the Chicago sky

B. Writing Sentences with Correct Capitalization

On the lines after each of the following items, write a brief sentence using a specific noun for each general noun given (and not at the beginning of the sentence).

EX.   team _____*My favorite team is Austin FC.*_____

1. aunt _____

_____

2. business _____

_____

3. institution _____

_____

4. religion _____

_____

5. nationality _____

_____

6. town or city _____

_____

7. country _____

_____

8. street _____

_____

9. region _____

_____

10. island _____

_____

11. forest or park _____

_____

12. mountains _____

_____

13. school subject _____

_____

14. a food modified with a proper adjective _____

_____

15. a body of water _____

_____

OBJECTS, EVENTS, AND AWARDS

12i   **Capitalize the brand names of business products.**

The names of the types of products are not capitalized.

EXAMPLES   **R**itz crackers, **C**olgate toothpaste, **K**leenex tissues

12j   **Capitalize the names of historical events and periods, special events, and calendar items.**

EXAMPLES   **G**reat **D**epression, **F**all of **R**ome, **R**estoration, **D**ark **A**ges, **R**oaring **T**wenties, **K**entucky **D**erby, **V**alentine's **D**ay, **T**uesday

12k   **Capitalize the names of ships, monuments, awards, planets, and any other particular places, things, or events.**

Type of Name	Examples
ships, trains	**HMS** *Frolic,* **B**roadway **L**imited
aircraft, spacecraft	**A**ir **F**orce **O**ne, **M**ars **G**lobal **S**urveyor
monuments, memorials	the **S**phinx, **J**efferson **M**emorial
awards	**E**mmy, **G**uggenheim **F**ellowship
planets, stars, constellations	**S**aturn, **P**hobos, **P**ole **S**tar, **S**corpius

NOTES   In addition to begin capitalized, names of ships (but not prefixes such as HMS or USS) are also set in italics.

Lowercase *sun* and *moon* and *earth*, except when *Earth* is used to name the planet.

EXAMPLES   **V**enus is the second planet from the **s**un; **E**arth is the third.
            The miners dug deep into the rocky **e**arth, searching for rare minerals.

EXERCISE 6   Proofreading Sentences for Correct Capitalization

For each of the following sentences, draw a line through each incorrectly capitalized word, and write the word correctly on the line below the sentence.

EX.   How many moons does the planet ~~jupiter~~ have?
       Jupiter

1.   Have you ever visited the Washington monument?

    _____

2.   The ferry *salem express* rammed a coral reef near Safaga, Egypt, in 1991.

    _____

3. Lupe's new laptop uses microsoft software.

_____

4. What events led up to the boston tea party?

_____

5. Mom has both memorial day and veterans day off from work.

_____

6. Someday your reporting work might earn you a pulitzer prize.

_____

7. People often play harmless pranks on april fools' day.

_____

8. F. Scott Fitzgerald was one of the famous writers of the jazz age.

_____

9. The planet venus has a surface temperature of about 887° F.

_____

10. One of the most advanced ships in the world is the U.S. Navy's USS *zumwalt*.

_____

11. For heroism on the battlefield, my uncle was awarded the medal of honor.

_____

12. Which occurred first, the french revolution or the american revolution?

_____

13. "At grand central station, you can get on the subway," she noted.

_____

14. In what year was the new york world's fair held?

_____

15. The closest star to our own sun is alpha centauri.

_____

16. The enlightenment was a period of scientific discovery and invention.

_____

17. Last wednesday, we viewed the rings of saturn through a telescope at a local observatory.

_____

18. Would you like to contribute money to support the special olympics?

_____

19. Maya uses only android phones.

_____

20. The constellation pegasus is named for a mythological horse with wings.

_____

TITLES

12l   Capitalize titles.

(1) Capitalize the title of a person when it comes before the person's name.

EXAMPLES   Did **Dr.** Vaidhyanathan write you a prescription?
Did **V**ice **P**resident Kamala Harris serve on the committee?

(2) Capitalize a word showing a family relationship when the word is used before or in place of a person's name but not when it is preceded by a possessive form.

EXAMPLES   **G**randpa and **A**unt Gwendolyn both play tennis.
Have I introduced you to my cousin Rigoberta?

(3) Capitalize the first and last words and all important words in titles of books, newspapers, magazines, poems, short stories, historical documents, movies, works of art, musical compositions, and television, radio, and podcast series and episodes.

Unimportant words in titles include articles (*a, an, the*), coordinating conjunctions (*and, but, for, nor, or, so, yet*), and prepositions (*at, for, from, with*).

NOTE   An article (*a, an,* or *the*) in a title is not capitalized unless it is the first word of the title.

Type of Title	Examples
books	*The Kitchen God's Wife, Searoad*
newspapers or magazines	*The New York Times, People*
poems	"Snake," "Not Waving but Drowning"
short stories	"Araby," "The Yellow Wallpaper"
historical documents	Treaty of Versailles, Mayflower Compact
movies	*The Fabelmans, Titanic*
television, radio, or podcast series and episodes	*Good Morning America, Jeopardy!, Let's Make a Sci-Fi*
works of art	*The Blue Boy, American Gothic*
musical compositions	"Go Down, Moses," *Sonata in E-flat*

NOTE   Use italics for titles of books, plays, periodicals, films, works of art, long musical works, and television, radio, and podcast series. Use quotation marks to enclose the titles of short works, such as short stories, poems, articles, songs, and individual television, radio, and podcast episodes.

EXERCISE 7   Proofreading for Correct Capitalization

For each sentence below, correct the errors in capitalization by drawing a line through each error and writing the correct form in the space above it. If a sentence is correct, write *C* above it.

>   *A*

EX.   Jaime did a report on the career of ~~a~~dmiral Chester W. Nimitz.

1. Afghan-American author Khaled Hosseini wrote *the Kite runner*.

2. I read an article about Montreal in *national geographic*.

3. My Mom asked Aunt Consuelo to edit the email for her.

4. Langston Hughes wrote the poem "blues at dawn."

5. *The wall street journal* is a popular newspaper among business people.

6. The television series *this is us* has won multiple Emmy Awards

7. Have you read Uri Orlev's book *the man from the other side*?

8. Dylan, you can see Dr. Sanchez now.

9. Paulo loves to watch the television show *the voice*.

10. We heard a moving performance of Brahms's *piano concerto no. 2*.

11. How many people signed the declaration of independence?

12. Have you seen *star wars, return of the jedi*, or *the empire strikes back?*

13. Thomas Friedman wrote the book *from Beirut to Jerusalem*.

14. The lecture on Indian women writers will be given by Professor Zenobia

     Battacherya.

15. "The *des moines register* is an excellent newspaper," said Maria.

16. The strategic arms reduction treaty was signed in 1991 by George H.W. Bush and

     Mikhail Gorbachev.

17. Did uncle Toshiro actually cook dinner for you?

18. Isaac Bashevis Singer wrote a fine short story called "the fatalist."

19. On September 29, 2005, Chief justice John G. Roberts Jr., took his place on the Supreme Court.

20. Carmen Lomas Garza's painting *birthday party for lala and tudi* shows children gathered around a piñata.

MODULE REVIEW

A.   Correcting Errors in Capitalization

For each sentence below, correct the errors in capitalization by drawing a line through the error and writing the correct form in the space above it.

>   *P*   *F*   *N*   *P*   *A*
> EX.   The ~~p~~etrified ~~f~~orest ~~n~~ational ~~p~~ark is in ~~a~~rizona.

1. Did you know that mount etna is an active volcano in italy?

2. Did you say eddie was a cashier at walmart?

3. There are two houses in parliament, the governing body of great britain.

4. My Father asked, "did you send that form to the irs?"

5. I would love to see rodin's *the thinker* at a museum.

6. I got information for that report from *the norton anthology of american literature.*

7. My brother Jeremiah bought McIntosh Apples at the new stop & shop grocery

    store last saturday.

8. Our neighbors are saving money to visit the great wall of china after thanksgiving.

9. uncle virgil's favorite collection of poems, *the rubáiyát,* was written by omar

    khayyám.

10. My spanish class meets every friday afternoon at 148 beacon street.

B.   Proofreading for Correct Capitalization

In the paragraph below, correct errors in capitalization by drawing a line through the error and writing the correct form in the space above it. If a sentence is correct, write *C* above it.

$$\overset{E}{}\qquad\overset{H}{}$$

EX.   My best friend ~~e~~milio is from ~~h~~onduras.

[1] Emilio showed me a photograph of the caribbean sea, which borders Honduras to the North. [2] His family moved to the united states two years ago on september 15, which is also independence day in Honduras. [3] Honduras got its independence from spain in 1821. [4] among the largest cities in Honduras is Tegucigalpa, which is the capital. [5] The area where this country lies was first inhabited by the Mayan civilization. [6] Native Peoples, the lenca, also made homes in this territory. [7] Today Honduras is mainly made up of mestizos and Native Peoples. [8] The country is a republic led by president xiomara castro. [9] The country is governed by the national congress, which has 128 members. [10] Honduras does most of its trading with the United States, and it is a member of the central american common market.

END MARKS

End marks—periods, question marks, and exclamation points—are used to indicate the purpose of a sentence.

13a   A statement (or declarative sentence) ends with a period.

EXAMPLE   Zena is washing the car**.**

When an abbreviation with a period is written at the end of a sentence, another period is not used as an end mark. However, a question mark or an exclamation point is used as needed.

EXAMPLES   Toni was just hired at Springfield Computers, Inc**.**
                         When does Toni start her new job at Springfield Computers, Inc.**?**

13b   A question (or interrogative sentence) ends with a question mark.

EXAMPLES   Did you ask for an application**?**
                         Whose lunch is this**?**

(1) Do not use a question mark after a declarative sentence stating an indirect question.

EXAMPLES   Mara wondered why elephants have tusks.
                         Jackson asked me if I knew how to play chess.

(2) A polite request in question form may be followed by either a period or a question mark.

EXAMPLES   Will you please complete this form**?**
                                          or
                         Will you please complete this form**.**

(3) If a quotation is a question, place the question mark inside the closing quotation marks. Otherwise, place it outside the closing quotation marks.

EXAMPLES   Mara asked, "Why do elephants have tusks**?**" [The quotation is a question.]
                         Did you hear me say "I don't know"**?** [The quotation is not a question.]

13c   An exclamation ends with an exclamation point.

EXAMPLES   How incredible that game was**!**   Oh my**!**   Wow**!**

(1) An interjection at the beginning of a sentence is usually followed by a comma. It may be followed by an exclamation point for greater emphasis.

EXAMPLES   Hey, quiet down!   or   Hey! Quiet down!

(2) If a quotation is an exclamation, place the exclamation mark inside the closing quotation marks. Otherwise, place it outside the closing quotation marks.

EXAMPLES   Taylor exclaimed, "Oh no!" [The quotation is an exclamation.]

                    I can't believe you said "OK"! [The quotation is not an exclamation.]

13d   An imperative sentence may end with either a period or an exclamation point.

EXAMPLES   Please listen to what I have to say. [a request]

                    Be quiet! [a command]

Sometimes a command is stated in question form. However, since its purpose is to give a command, it should be followed by an exclamation point.

EXAMPLE   Will you just wait a minute!

EXERCISE 1   Correcting Sentences by Adding End Marks

Add the proper end mark to each of the sentences below.

    EX.   Are we there yet?

1. That's amazing
2. Frank asked, "What's for dinner"
3. Whose pile of laundry is this
4. Sarah asked why we don't visit her more often
5. Last night, Sergio balanced an egg on his nose
6. Are you going to Makayla's graduation party
7. This town enforces its speed limits
8. Run, Julia, run
9. Gianna put on her jacket and walked away
10. How is Mr. Joseph's condition today
11. Don't you dare tell
12. Did you hear Sophia say, "Thank you"
13. Miriam yelled, "Yikes"
14. Will you just forget it
15. We asked Rudy about his job interview

ABBREVIATIONS

13e **An abbreviation is usually followed by a period.**

Abbreviations with Periods	
Personal Names	E. L. Doctorow, Sally K. Ride
Titles Used with Names	Dr., Jr., Sr., Mr., Mrs., Ms.
Organizations and Companies	Co., Inc., Corp.
Addresses	St., Rd., Ave., Blvd.
Times of Day, Days, Months	a.m., p.m., Tues., Oct.
Abbreviations Without Periods	
Government Agencies	FBI, CIA, FDA, NASA
State Abbreviations	AZ, CT, HI, IA, NE, PA, TX, WA
Units of Measure (metric)	cm, kg, ml, g (*or* gm)
Widely Used Abbreviations	EPA, PBS, PTA, NAACP, UNICEF, BCE, CE, PO Box

NOTE   Two-letter state codes are not followed by periods.

   EXAMPLES   Kansas City, **MO** 64131   New Orleans, **LA** 70115

NOTE   In most cases, an abbreviation is capitalized only if the words that it stands for are capitalized. If you are unsure whether to use periods with an abbreviation or whether to capitalize it, check a dictionary.

EXERCISE 2   Proofreading for Correct Punctuation of Abbreviations

In the items below, add or delete periods where needed. If an item is correct, write *C* above it.

   EX.   6:45 a.m.

1. Eugene, OR 97404

2. Dr Ivan Ivanovich

3. 12 oz

4. 2 kg.

5. NBA

6. Luisa Gutierrez, D.D.S.

7. SPCA

8. 11:30 p m

9. Little Rock, A.R.

10. National Governors Assn

REVIEW EXERCISE

A.   Correcting Punctuation in Sentences

In the sentences below, add periods, question marks, and exclamation points where needed.

EX.   She addressed the invitation to Dr. Ruth B. Epstein.

1. The 10-lb package was mistakenly shipped to Fargo, ND

2. Could you see the lunar eclipse after 10:00 pm

3. Why do we have to leave so early for the Howard St station

4. Ace Co and Competent Corp were cited as up-and-coming U S businesses

5. Did Mr Elliott really have an interview with the F.B.I. at 8 am

6. According to the story I heard, Constance caught a 14-in trout

7. We've recently moved to 138 Ash St, Portland, O.R.

8. The F.C.C issued new rules for smartphones.

9. Dr Fisk said the baby weighed exactly 3 kg. at birth

10. The tournament was in Madison, WI

B.   Writing Notes

Suddenly this morning, thousands of letters, postcards, and packages started falling from the sky! You cautiously investigate this mail storm and write a blog post about it. Write five sentences about what is happening. Use all three types of end marks and two abbreviations in your sentences.

EX.   *A mail storm is paralyzing the town of Greenville, SC.*
       Witnesses reported this strange event started at 5:30 a.m.

_____

_____

_____

_____

_____

_____

_____

_____

COMMAS IN A SERIES

13f   Use commas to separate items in a series.

WORDS   I am going to the lecture with Maurice, Loretta, Candace, and Mauricio.

PHRASES   We put up campaign posters in the main hall, in the cafeteria, in the gym, and near the concession stand.

CLAUSES   The counselor said that I had worked hard, that I had completed all the make-up assignments, and that I could play with the team again.

Some paired words—such as *macaroni and cheese,* or *peanut butter and jelly*—may be considered a single item.

EXAMPLE   Tasha had milk, peanut butter and jelly, and carrots for lunch.

NOTE   If all items in a series are joined by *and, or,* or *nor,* do not separate them with commas.

EXAMPLES   This smoothie contains mango **and** kale **and** orange juice.

Would you prefer to ride along the eastern shore **or** the western shore **or** over the hill into Owl Valley?

13g   Use commas to separate two or more adjectives that describe the same noun, unless the adjectives do not modify the same noun equally.

EXAMPLES   Heidi is a steady, experienced, highly skilled golfer.

My brother really likes the funny trucker hat we got him for his birthday.

NOTE   Try inserting *and* between the adjectives in a series. If *and* fits sensibly, use a comma. For example, *steady, experienced,* and *highly skilled* sounds sensible, so a comma is used. *And* cannot be logically inserted in *funny trucker hat,* however.

EXERCISE 3   Proofreading Sentences for the Correct Use of Commas

Insert commas where needed in the sentences below. If a sentence is correct, write *C* on the line before the sentence.

EX. _____   Green orange and purple are the secondary colors.

_____   1. On Tuesday, Martin misplaced his books his wallet and his phone.

_____   2. Every morning, Darren enjoys oatmeal wheat toast with peanut butter and juice.

_____ 3. Before chewing the couch, the puppy ate my slippers my gloves and my brother's hat.

_____ 4. The leaves on the tree are orange and maroon and red.

_____ 5. Marco and Marie named their four children Martha Mary Marsha and Michael.

_____ 6. I'm hungry for breakfast, but I can't decide whether to eat yogurt or eggs and toast.

_____ 7. The decorations committee hung balloons in the cafeteria in the gymnasium and above the lockers in the hall.

_____ 8. Franklin, Yoshi and James are my three best friends.

_____ 9. I'm not sure if we're going to a movie or to a play this Saturday night.

_____ 10. Many of the plays performed at this theater were written by well-known playwrights such as Wasserstein Gurira Stoppard and Mamet.

_____ 11. Exercising three times a week eating a balanced diet and drinking water can help with well-being.

_____ 12. They say she is a dedicated experienced and energetic leader.

_____ 13. Gary and Ricardo and Che visited Lionel over the weekend.

_____ 14. Nobody knew who the contest winners were when they had been selected or when they would be announced.

_____ 15. My little brother's favorite foods are rice macaroni and cheese and bananas.

_____ 16. The critic hailed the author's latest mystery novel as "Clever suspenseful wicked and wonderful!"

_____ 17. Go to the corner of West End and 76th Street turn right onto 76th and walk three blocks to our apartment.

_____ 18. Carmen enjoys her classes in history, math, and science.

_____ 19. Thank you for the lovely evening the delicious dinner and the exquisite dessert.

_____ 20. Choose any of these colors: green yellow blue red.

COMMAS WITH INDEPENDENT CLAUSES

13h Use commas before *and, but, for, nor, or, so,* and *yet* when they join independent clauses.

EXAMPLE   Prajit said he enjoyed the book**, but** Adelita said she thought the writing was awkward.

The word *for* is now used as a conjunction only in formal situations. Only use a comma before *for* when it is sued as a conjunction combining two independent clauses. Do not use a comma before *for* when it is used as a preposition.

PREP (no comma)   CONJ (comma)

EXAMPLE   The decorations **for** the party should be replaced**, for** the wind has blown them down.

NOTE   Always use a comma before *for, so,* and *yet* when they join independent clauses. However, before *and, but, nor,* and *or,* the comma may be omitted if the clauses are very short and if there is no possibility of misunderstanding their meanings.

CORRECT   I waited **but** nobody else showed up.
INCORRECT   I waited with Clara and Lars and Yoko searched.
CORRECT   I waited with Clara**, and** Lars and Yoko searched.

Do not confuse a compound sentence with a simple sentence that has a compound verb.

SIMPLE SENTENCE   I raked the leaves **and** loaded them into the barrel. [one independent clause with a compound verb]
COMPOUND SENTENCE   I raked the leaves**, and** I loaded them into the barrel. [two independent clauses]

EXERCISE 4   Correcting Punctuation in Sentences by Adding Commas

For each of the following sentences, insert commas where needed. If a sentence is correct, write *C* on the line before the sentence.

EX. _____   Mara folded the towels**,** and her brother ironed the shirts.

_____   1. Yukio explained her reasoning but Charles wasn't listening.

_____   2. The oranges were large and plump yet the apples looked more refreshing.

_____   3. I called the box office but the concert was already sold-out.

_____   4. Una smiled and held out two invitations.

_____ 5. The sculptor did not want the clay to dry so he covered it with a damp cloth.

_____ 6. Everyone was offered a choice of rice or potatoes yet many people asked for couscous.

_____ 7. In the attic, Emily found old letters stored in shoeboxes and she didn't know what to do with them.

_____ 8. Lexi usually enjoys ice skating or skiing but the weather is too warm this winter.

_____ 9. Jamal studied the photographer's technique for he wanted to learn the process.

_____ 10. Rowan suggests that I plant marigolds around the garden or pests will invade the tomatoes again.

_____ 11. The sky darkened and everyone knew a storm or tornado was approaching.

_____ 12. Adele and Ted enjoyed the book but they didn't want to see the film adaptation.

_____ 13. Xavier was tired after two hours of shoveling snow yet he cleared his neighbor's sidewalk, too.

_____ 14. Odessa is a person's name and it is also the name of a place.

_____ 15. Is the Coliseum in Paris or is it in Rome?

_____ 16. My math teacher says my work is improving but she thinks I need better study habits.

_____ 17. We looked at the Roman drawings and sculptures and then we compared them with modern works.

_____ 18. Finally, the children took a nap but they didn't stay asleep for long.

_____ 19. Vanya completed the experiment and developed her notes into a lab report.

_____ 20. Ivan and Ben spoke different languages yet that was not a barrier to their friendship.

13i **Use commas to set off nonessential participial phrases and nonessential clauses.**

A *nonessential* (or *nonrestrictive*) participial phrase or clause is one containing information that is not needed to understand the main idea of the sentence.

NONESSENTIAL PHRASES	The runner, **hampered by the injury,** did not do as well as expected.
	Aretha Cao, **having passed the bar examination,** is now an attorney.
NONESSENTIAL CLAUSES	Joey Fox, **who completed his lap in the relay,** passed the baton beautifully.
	My cousin's farm, **which is in eastern Washington,** is a great place to visit.

Each nonessential clause or phrase in the examples above could be omitted without changing the main idea of the sentence.

EXAMPLES	The runner did not do as well as expected.
	Aretha Cao is now an attorney.
	Joey Fox passed the baton beautifully.
	My cousin's farm is a great place to visit.

An *essential* (or *restrictive*) clause or phrase is not set off by commas because it contains information that is necessary to the meaning of the sentence.

ESSENTIAL PHRASES	The man **feeding the pigeons** did not notice us.
	The film **scheduled for Friday** has been cancelled.
ESSENTIAL CLAUSES	We hired a lawyer **who is named Al Hopkins.**
	Anyone **who solves the puzzle** will win a prize.

Notice how omitting the essential phrase or clause changes the main idea of the sentence.

EXAMPLES	The man did not notice us.
	The film has been cancelled.
	We hired a lawyer.
	Anyone will win a prize.

NOTE	Adjective clauses beginning with *that* are nearly always essential.	
	EXAMPLE	Please return the book **that I lent you last month**.

EXERCISE 5　Correcting Sentences by Adding Commas

For each of the sentences below, identify the italicized phrase or clause by writing *E* for *essential* or *NE* for *nonessential* on the line before the sentence. Insert commas where needed.

EX. __*NE*__　The finch, *watched by the cat*, flew to a higher branch.

_____ 1. Monday *which is my sister's birthday* is the first day of school.

_____ 2. The dog *covered with fleas* would not stop scratching.

_____ 3. Alice Munro *who is my favorite author* is from Canada.

_____ 4. I enjoy a tomato sauce *that tastes fresh and tangy*.

_____ 5. The trout *which had been caught by Uncle Bob* was served for dinner.

_____ 6. After Alisha talks to the petsitter *who is our neighbor* she'll be ready to leave.

_____ 7. This park *known for its orchid hybrids* has a new groundskeeper.

_____ 8. I gave Jennie the birthday gift *that her father suggested*.

_____ 9. Any photographs *needing to be framed* must be turned in this morning.

_____ 10. Amanda was determined to learn Spanish, a language *that had always interested her*.

_____ 11. Hector washed his little brother's face *which was covered with peanut butter*.

_____ 12. The staff *excited by the promise of a holiday* worked even harder.

_____ 13. Tell Maxine *that the new movie has a thrilling and complex plot*.

_____ 14. Jasmine *who had excelled in science* has been nominated for a major award.

_____ 15. Brussels sprouts *which look like tiny cabbages* flourish in cool weather.

_____ 16. The writer *frustrated by the neighbor's loud music* did not complete the manuscript on time.

_____ 17. Any detective *who solves the mystery* will be promoted.

_____ 18. My new puppies *who are named Stefan and Tasha* make me feel energetic.

_____ 19. Natalie Beltoya *whose parents are from Belarus* fluently speaks three languages.

_____ 20. We were amazed that the architect *pressured by construction deadlines* completed the building on schedule.

MODULE 13: PUNCTUATION

COMMAS WITH INTRODUCTORY ELEMENTS

13j **Use a comma after introductory elements.**

(1) Use a comma after mild exclamations, such as *well* **or** *why,* **and after other introductory words such as** *yes* **and** *no.*

EXAMPLES   **Oh,** didn't you know anyone else was here?

                Why, I think I'll just go for a walk.

                Yes, you may accompany me if you prefer.

(2) Use a comma after an introductory participial phrase.

EXAMPLES   **Peeking around the corner,** she spied the woman with the briefcase.

                Buried in the yard, the iron post began to rust.

(3) Use a comma after an introductory prepositional phrase.

EXAMPLES   **After lunch,** I brush my teeth.

                In the morning before school, I practice for my piano lessons.

                In the watering can on the shelf beneath the stairs, I've hidden my diary.

(4) Use a comma after an introductory adverb clause.

An introductory adverb clause may appear at the beginning of a sentence or before any independent clause in the sentence.

EXAMPLES   **As I look back,** I can see that I made a few mistakes.

                I only hope that **when we finally get there,** there will still be some watermelon left.

EXERCISE 6   Proofreading Sentences for Correct Use of Commas

For each of the following sentences, insert commas where needed. If a sentence is correct, write *C* on the line before the sentence.

    EX. _____   On the shelf in the back entry**,** a clutter of dog leashes, sticks, and frisbees is assembled.

_____ 1. No we do not wish to order dinner yet.

_____ 2. Covered completely with dust the bookshelves, cabinets, and chairs revealed neglect.

_____ 3. Hey did you hear Juanita's good news?

_____ 4. Scratching at the carpet the old dog tried to bury an imaginary bone.

_____ 5. On the shelf behind the cookbooks I've hidden Evan's birthday gift.

_____ 6. When they called I met them at the airport.

_____ 7. After her morning shower Alisha feels alert, awake, and ready to go.

_____ 8. Holding the model in her hands Maxine dreamed about planes she'd fly someday.

_____ 9. Until the rooster crowed not even the cows mooed.

_____ 10. Maybe but let's see what happens next.

_____ 11. In a low valley under a pine tree they finally pitched their tent for the night.

_____ 12. Swinging their arms they happily walked along the beach.

_____ 13. After the first phone call the office jumps to life.

_____ 14. Quick as ever the juggler tossed a dozen tomatoes into the air and caught them.

_____ 15. Dressed in brightly colored costumes we danced in the streets at Mardi Gras.

_____ 16. Yes I got your message.

_____ 17. Anxious that David was late Luis called David's parents.

_____ 18. After the guests had left and throughout the rest of the night they washed dishes.

_____ 19. Well I don't really know what to think.

_____ 20. Having sung the aria the diva left the stage.

_____ 21. At the base of the mountain in a cave a reclusive miner keeps his home.

_____ 22. Thanking all of the volunteers the radio announcer finally ended the fund drive.

_____ 23. Wow is it ever cold out here!

_____ 24. Okay but let's meet at the movies anyway.

_____ 25. After she found her tickets Amelia put on her coat, locked the door, and hurried to the airport.

COMMAS WITH OTHER SENTENCE INTERRUPTERS

13k   Use commas to set off elements that interrupt the sentence.

(1) Use commas to set off appositives and appositive phrases.

An *appositive* is a noun or pronoun that follows another noun or pronoun to identify or explain it. An *appositive phrase* consists of an appositive and its modifiers.

EXAMPLES   Young at Heart, **a toy store,** has some part-time openings.
Both of them, **he and his brother,** helped me fix my ten-speed.

In some cases, an appositive tells which one of multiple options is meant. Such **essential appositives** are not set off with commas. Notice the difference in these examples.

ESSENTIAL   My dog Max likes to swim in the lake more than my dog Fluffy does. [The speaker has more than one dog, so the appositives are essential to the meaning of the sentence.]

NONESSENTIAL   My cat, Charlie, likes to sit by the window. [The speaker has only one cat, so omitting the appositive would not change the meaning.]

(2) Use commas to set off words used in direct address.

EXAMPLES   **Ilya,** have you seen my gloves?
Your car, **Abel,** has the largest bumpers I've ever seen.
Is there no end to your surprises, **Di**?

(3) Use commas to set off parenthetical expressions.

Parenthetical expressions are remarks that add incidental information or relate ideas to each other.

Commonly Used Parenthetical Expressions		
after all	I believe (hope, etc.)	naturally
at any rate	incidentally	nevertheless
by the way	in fact	of course
consequently	in general	on the contrary
for example	in the first place	on the other hand
for instance	meanwhile	that is
however	morever	therefore

EXAMPLES **After all,** you did say to make the banner large.
I did not, **however,** give you permission to use the living room.
It was the only room large enough for our meeting, **of course**.

Some of these expressions are not always parenthetical. When not used parenthetically, they should not be set off by commas.

EXAMPLES **In the first place,** we already have a car. [used parenthetically]
He found the ring **in the first place** he looked. [not parenthetical]

NOTE A contrasting expression introduced by *not* or *yet* is parenthetical and should also be set off by commas.

EXAMPLES It was at Alyssa's birthday party, **not mine,** that you sang for the group.
These boots are tight, **yet not too tight.**

EXERCISE 7   Correcting Sentences by Adding Commas

For each of the sentences below, insert commas where needed. If a sentence is correct, write *C* on the line before the sentence.

EX. _____ In general, we try to go to sleep before midnight.

_____ 1. Your cat by the way seems quite friendly.

_____ 2. In fact Victor flew to Dallas last week.

_____ 3. Carole have you seen the book that I was reading?

_____ 4. Frank's mother an engineer likes the household to run smoothly.

_____ 5. Haley's lab partner Terry wrote the conclusion to their report.

_____ 6. Parsley the best-growing plant in our garden is often nibbled to its roots by birds.

_____ 7. Our parakeet Hubert is named after one of our friends.

_____ 8. I wonder Thomas when you'll bring us good news.

_____ 9. That shade of purple looks terrific on you Latisha.

_____ 10. Nevertheless Anna Brown the class president asked for a vote recount.

_____ 11. For example I study after school with Jamal a math tutor.

_____ 12. My friend Ha-Yoon is much better at playing soccer than all my other friends.

_____ 13. Finn's work in history class though often late shows a lot of insight.

_____ 14. My brother said, "Nick you need a haircut."

_____ 15. I framed the photo I took of my mother's cat Gertrude.

MODULE 13: PUNCTUATION
OTHER USES OF COMMAS

13l   **Use a comma to separate items in dates and addresses.**

EXAMPLES   I was born on Friday, **July 1, 2004,** in this small hospital.

Write to me at 1609 Sunny Dale St., **Oak Creek, WI 53154,** after the first of March.

Notice that commas are not placed between the month and the day, between the house number and the street name, or between the two-letter state code and the ZIP Code. Notice also that a comma separates the final item in a date and in an address from the words that follow it.

13m   **Use a comma after the salutation of a friendly letter and after the closing of any letter.**

EXAMPLES   Dear Moira,   Yours sincerely,

13n   **Do not use unnecessary commas.**

Use a comma only when a rule requires one or if the meaning is unclear without one.

INCORRECT   The movie camera that I borrowed from the equipment room, is the one I used. [*Camera* is the subject; it must not be separated from its verb *is*.]

CORRECT   The movie camera that I borrowed from the equipment room is the one I used.

EXERCISE 8   Correcting Sentences by Adding Commas

For each of the following sentences, insert commas where needed. If a sentence is correct, write *C* on the line before the sentence.

EX. _____   On Friday, June 2, school lets out early.

_____   1.   After writing the letter, she signed it, "Sincerely yours Odessa."

_____   2.   My dental appointment is on Friday August 18 2023.

_____   3.   He lived at 110 Cactus Court Albuquerque New Mexico for ten years.

_____   4.   Someone that you haven't heard from in a while called today.

_____   5.   The invitation read, "Dear Alani Please join us for dinner on Saturday."

_____ 6. A young researcher made the discovery at the University of Rochester in Rochester New York.

_____ 7. Seattle Washington is considered a desirable place to live.

_____ 8. I heard that Sharon arrives next Saturday March 14 on the train.

_____ 9. He wrote a letter of complaint to 22 Stratosphere Lane Jupiter.

_____ 10. On August 21 2022 we had a wonderful picnic.

_____ 11. The nearest fruit market is located at Highway 30 Racine Wisconsin.

_____ 12. The boy in our class named Achebe is from Nigeria.

_____ 13. Our next meeting will be at 30 Cedar Street Davenport IA 52803.

_____ 14. The store no longer stocks the shampoo that I usually buy.

_____ 15. After turning right at the corner, you'll find 500 Orangewood Place Eugene Oregon on your left.

MODULE 13: PUNCTUATION
MODULE REVIEW

A. Proofreading Sentences for Correct Punctuation

For each of the following sentences, insert commas and end marks where needed. Draw a line through any commas or periods that are unnecessary. If a sentence is correct, write C on the line before the sentence.

EX. ___*C*___ Wide-eyed, eager, and alert, we began our great adventure.

_____ 1. Quick throw the ball to Hank

_____ 2. Una played the flute and the violin and the drums.

_____ 3. Charles Washington my neighbor lives down the block at 7500 Paulina Street

_____ 4. She signed the letter, "Yours truly Veronica I Smith."

_____ 5. Were you born on March 1 2007 or March 7 2001

_____ 6. The talk show guest who was a famous athlete announced his retirement, and spoke of his future plans.

_____ 7. Rory ironed the shirts pants and skirts; and Hollis folded the last load of clothes from the dryer.

_____ 8. Hot, and sweaty, and tired they pulled dozens of weeds from the garden

_____ 9. Taking the bench the judge looked at the jury cleared her throat and asked if they had reached a decision yet.

_____ 10. Do you know if F.B.I. stands for Federal Bureau of Investigation

_____ 11. She wondered if Stefan heard her but he didn't.

_____ 12. After our visit to Grandma's farm, the city's smog seemed thicker.

_____ 13. Ms Schumann a promising scientist prefers to spend her holidays reading adventure novels

_____ 14. Running ahead of the other dogs the boxer caught the stick that I threw

_____ 15. Well you could have fooled me

_____ 16. Eager to be at sea the young sailors volunteered their services aboard the steamer *Argos* and they leave tomorrow.

_____ 17. For example if Jim Jr comes home early you can bet soccer practice will be canceled

_____ 18. Energetic and strong the gymnast who was last year's silver medalist won the gold

_____ 19. Henry before those muffins burn take the pan out of the oven

_____ 20. The sweater that I bought yesterday is too large.

B.   Proofreading a Paragraph for Correct Punctuation

In the paragraph below, add end marks and commas where needed. Draw a line through any punctuation marks that are misplaced. If a sentence is correct, write *C* on the line before the sentence.

EX. _____ What is so unusual about bonsai, those small trees?

_____ [1] Bonsai small ornamental trees are grown in low shallow

pots. _____ [2] Very slow growers they are shaped over a long period of

time _____ [3] For example one of the bonsai a dwarf maple is over fifty

years old. _____ [4] Some bonsai if cared for tenderly, and properly live

to be hundreds of years old _____ [5] These bonsai, passed down from

one generation to another, are rare and valuable.

14a **Use a semicolon to join two closely related independent clauses.**

EXAMPLE   Dominic had won his heat; he caught his breath and drank some water before the finals.

14b **Use a semicolon between independent clauses joined by a conjunctive adverb or transitional expression that is followed by a comma.**

EXAMPLE   Hannah decided not to audition for the play; **instead,** she applied to be stage manager.

Landry and Rory studied diligently for the test; **as a result,** their grades improved.

14c **Use a semicolon (rather than a comma) between independent clauses joined by a coordinating conjunction when the clauses contain commas.**

EXAMPLE   To prepare for the meeting, Andy arranged the chairs around the conference table; he laid a fresh notepad, a pencil, and a cup of water at each place; and then he set up a microphone for the speaker, Mr. Foster Kern of the Tennessee Industrial Council.

14d **Use a colon before a list of items, especially after such expressions as *as follows* and *the following.***

EXAMPLES For her talk to the class, Rebecca planned to use several visual props: a series of photographs, two posters, and a short video.

Those applying for the voc-tech school scholarship must submit **the following:** a completed application form, two letters of reference, and photographs or samples of their best work.

14e **Use a colon before a long, formal statement or quotation.**

EXAMPLE   Although Mom was so surprised that she could hardly speak, she finally said: "Thank you all for coming and making my fiftieth birthday so special. I love you all. And thank you, whoever planned this surprise party for me. I am just so touched by all of this."

14f **Use a colon between independent clauses when the second clause explains or restates the idea of the first, or between a title and its subtitle.**

EXAMPLES Gabriel and many of his friends were late for school: They were on their way when the school bus's transmission seized up, and then they had to wait for another bus to pick them up.

Genealogy: A Practical Research Guide [book title]

EXERCISE 1   Proofreading Sentences for Correct Use of Semicolons and Colons

The sentences below are missing semicolons and colons. In each sentence, write the missing punctuation mark where it is needed. If a sentence is correct, write *C* above it.

EX.   Terence said nothing; he didn't want to give any hints about the surprise party.

1. Wylie decided to cut his hair it had started to hang over his eyes.

2. The coach called a time out, and he told the team which play to run then he sent in a substitute for Kramer.

3. Arianna is no longer on the cheerleading squad instead, she stays after school to catch up on her classwork.

4. We rarely buy bread anymore we have been making it ourselves at home.

5. Paquito put on an apron, hot mitt, and chef's hat then he asked us if we wanted red, orange, or green peppers in our omelettes.

6. Their book was titled *Dimensions of Tolerance: What Americans Believe About Civil Liberties.*

7. When you arrive at Camp Apex, be sure you have brought the following items towels, shampoo, insect repellent, rain gear.

8. The burglar seemed to know exactly where the alarm system was how he knew is still a mystery.

9. Feeling tired, I took a hot bath I had a light snack and I went to bed early.

10. Dorotea was staying up all night Her government term paper was due the next day, and she had barely begun to work on it.

11. I am certainly much too clumsy to perform in public nevertheless, I enjoy dancing so much that I had to audition.

12. "Your oral reports will be graded on the following points organization, clarity, completeness, and audience interest," the teacher informed us.

13. Mr. Mori said in his speech "Ladies and gentlemen, we are here tonight to honor a distinguished co-worker and longtime friend."

14. Mario invited me to his home he's got a new math game for the computer.

15. Kibbe loved his home however, he also wanted to visit new places.

OTHER MARKS OF PUNCTUATION

14g   Use a hyphen

- with compound numbers from twenty-one to ninety-nine and with fractions used as modifiers
- with a compound adjective when it precedes the word it modifies
- with the prefixes *ex-, self-, all-,* and *great-*; with the suffixes *-elect,* and *-free*; and with all prefixes before a proper noun or proper adjective
- to prevent confusion or awkwardness

EXAMPLES   forty-eight actors
a well-written poem
ex-president
re-sign the contract

14h   Use a dash to indicate an abrupt break in thought.

EXAMPLES   My dad expects me to finish my homework on a typewriter—a manual typewriter!

Our coach made the decision—a big mistake—to use our last time-out with five minutes to play.

14i   Use a dash to mean *namely, in other words, that is,* and similar expressions that come before an explanation.

EXAMPLE   I made this cake for the reason I told you—tomorrow is Katrina's birthday.

14j   Use parentheses to enclose information that helps clarify or explain and material of minor importance.

EXAMPLES   The movie *Black Panther* (directed by Ryan Coogler) was a box-office success.

Bangladesh (formerly called East Pakistan) declared itself an independent nation in 1971.

14k   Use ellipsis points (. . .) to mark omissions from quoted material and pauses in a written passage.

(1) If the quoted material that comes before the omission is not a complete sentence, use three ellipsis points with a space before the first point.

EXAMPLE   De Luca writes, "I never felt threatened . . . when confronted by a great white shark."

(2) If the quoted material that comes before the omission is a complete sentence, keep the end mark and add the ellipsis points.

EXAMPLE   De Luca writes, "I never felt threatened . . . when confronted by a great white shark. . . . It could have been fatal. But I was careful."

(3) If one or more than one sentence is omitted, the ellipsis points follow the end mark that precedes the omission.

EXAMPLE   De Luca writes, "I never felt threatened . . . when confronted by a great white shark. . . . But I was careful."

(4) To indicate a pause in a written passage, use three ellipsis points with a space before the first point.

EXAMPLE   "Well, . . . I guess I could try," Marc replied.

NOTE   You may use other punctuation on either side of the ellipsis points if it helps to make sense of what has been omitted.

EXAMPLES   For example, . . . do not fold the cover.
Joel wrote . . . "We should all be proud."

EXERCISE 2   Using Hyphens Correctly

Add hyphens to the groups of words below that need them.

EX.   a much appreciated gesture
a much-appreciated gesture

1. her ex husband

2. a four fifths majority

3. a self fulfilling prophecy

4. a felt lined jacket

5. twenty senators elect

6. a noise free atmosphere

7. one fourth cup of molasses

8. their great grandmother

9. a much admired teenager

10. an all American basketball player

EXERCISE 3   Correcting Sentences with Dashes, Parentheses, and Ellipsis Points

In each of the following sentences, add the missing punctuation.

EX.   Be sure to use the proper form for your letter. (See page 27).

1. Vincente considered. "Well, . . I'm not so sure about that."

2. I said that what was mine was hers not that I had much to give.

3. The author made one character say, "Yikes . . Now I have nowhere to go!"

4. The team held a players-only meeting they were determined to end their losing streak right after practice.

5. The new rule is you probably already heard this everyone has to wear a shirt with a collar.

6. Dr. Seuss his real name is Theodor Geisel also wrote under the pseudonym Theo. LeSieg.

7. The quarterback I can't think of his name threw six touchdown passes.

8. Former U.S. senator John Glenn 1921—2016 first gained fame as an astronaut.

9. "I think I hear . . something in the basement," Tai whispered.

10. Some of the other students Lula and Esteban, for example have already begun their third project.

MODULE 14: PUNCTUATION

ITALICS

Italics are printed characters that slant to the right. To indicate italics in handwritten or typewritten work, use underlining.

14l **Use italics for titles of books, plays, periodicals (magazines and newspapers), films, television, radio, and podcast series, works of art, long musical compositions, and names of ships.**

Type of Name	Examples
Books	*The Fixer, A House of My Own*
Plays	*Driving Miss Daisy, The Piano Lesson*
Periodicals	*Sacramento Bee, New Republic*
Films	*The Matrix, Beauty and the Beast*
Television, Radio, and Podcast Series	*American Idol, The Tonight Show, Freakonomics Radio*
Works of Art	*No. 1: The Artist's Mother, The Storm*
Long Musical Compositions	*Third Symphony, Pagliacci*
Ships	USS *Lexington, Lusitania*

NOTE   Italicize the title of a poem only if the poem is long enough to be published in a separate volume. Such long poems are usually divided into titled or numbered sections. The titles of these sections are enclosed in quotation marks. Names of trains, aircraft, spacecraft, and space programs are capitalized but not italicized. Do not capitalize the letters USS before the name of a ship.

14m **Italicize foreign words as well as words, letters, and figures referred to as such.**

EXAMPLES   There are two *a*'s and two *e*'s in *separate*.

I can't tell whether this is an *a* or an *e*.

The abbreviation *etc.* stands for the Latin words *et cetera,* which mean "and so on."

EXERCISE 4   Correcting Sentences by Adding Underlining (Italics)

In the sentences below, underline each word or item that should be italicized. If a sentence is correct, write *C* above it.

EX.   I guess Chaucer's <u>Canterbury Tales</u> is the longest poem I've ever read.

1.   Jordan Peele has made a lot of movies with very short titles, including Get Out, Us, and Nope.

2.   My favorite Alicia Keys album is Girl on Fire. What's yours?

3.   When I want to watch old television shows, I always look for NOVA.

4.   The musical play The Wiz was based on the film The Wizard of Oz.

5.   My neighbor is a photographer for the Des Moines Register.

6.   The first steam-powered ship to cross the Atlantic was the Savannah in 1818.

7.   Fraktur is the German name for the fancy typeface that somewhat resembles Gothic script.

8.   My dad and I watched the series Stranger Things together.

9.   I plan to read The Fault in Our Stars before I see the film version.

10. There's a reproduction of Trumbull's painting The Declaration of Independence in my civics book.

11. The world's largest submarine, the USS Triton, is over sixty years old.

12. What have you learned about Michael Collins, one of the astronauts on Apollo 11?

13. Can you tell me the difference between whoever and whomever?

14. This book, What Color is Your Parachute, is about getting a job, but it also helps you learn about yourself.

15. The movie Beethoven's 2nd uses a 2, not two, in the title.

16. If you were famous, would you rather have your picture on the cover of Vanity Fair or the National Enquirer?

17. Two of the most popular plays on Broadway have been Hamilton and Phantom of the Opera.

18. It seems odd that the word glamor can also be spelled glamour.

19. Although it has no rhyme, Homer's epic Iliad is written in verse.

20. My three-year-old sister Uma called her clay blob Penguins at School.

APOSTROPHES

14n   Use an apostrophe to form the possessive of nouns and some pronouns.

(1) To form the possessive of a singular noun, add an apostrophe and an *s*.

EXAMPLES   the teacher**'s** pencil   Franklin**'s** clarinet
the desk**'s** surface   love**'s** simplicity

NOTE   To form the possessive of a singular noun ending in an *s* sound, add only an apostrophe if the noun has two or more syllables and if adding *'s* will make the word awkward to pronounce. Otherwise, add *'s*.

EXAMPLES   Mars**'s** atmosphere   Thomas**'s** vest
amaryllis**'** scent   for goodness**'** sake
Odysseus**'** travels   Paris**'** museums

(2) To form the possessive of a plural noun ending in *s*, add only the apostrophe.

EXAMPLES   the planets**'** orbits   the Mosses**'** house
maple trees**'** roots   the Wildcats**'** locker room

The few plural nouns that do not end in *s* form the possessive by adding *'s*.

EXAMPLES   teeth**'s** enamel   children**'s** story hour

NOTE   Do not use an apostrophe to form the plural of a noun.

INCORRECT   Some of these nail's are bent.
CORRECT   Some of these **nails** are bent.

(3) Do not use an apostrophe with possessive personal pronouns or with the possessive pronoun *whose*.

INCORRECT   Do you know it's weight?   That pen is her's.
CORRECT   Do you know **its** weight?   That pen is **hers.**

(4) To form the possessive of an indefinite pronoun, add an apostrophe and an *s*.

EXAMPLES   **Everyone's** dog must be leashed.
I want to see **everybody's** essay on time.

Form the possessive of such forms as *anyone else* and *somebody else* by adding an apostrophe and an *s*.

EXAMPLES   anyone else**'s**   anybody else**'s**   someone else**'s**

(5) To form the possessive of a hyphenated word, the name of an organization or a business firm, or a word in a group showing joint possession, add 's or an apostrophe only to the last word.

EXAMPLES   mother-in-law**'s** apartment   Acme Hardware**'s** sale

                   Lewis and Clark**'s** expedition   Fey and Poehler**'s** comedy sketch

(6) To show individual possession of similar items by each noun in a word group, add 's or an apostrophe only to each noun in the group.

EXAMPLE   Jared**'s**, Dalila**'s**, Jewel**'s**, and Paco**'s** campaign posters were all convincing.

(7) Use an apostrophe to form the possessive of words that indicate time or that indicate an amount in cents or dollars.

EXAMPLES   five **minutes'** rest   a full **day's** work

                   a **year's** time   a **dollar's** worth

EXERCISE 5   Forming Possessive Nouns and Pronouns

Each item below expresses possession by means of a prepositional phrase. Rewrite each item to express the same possession using a possessive noun or pronoun instead of a preposition.

EX.   blare of the trumpets
      trumpets' blare

1. march of the toy soldiers _____

2. the hat of Charles _____

3. the weather of the season _____

4. the main idea of it _____

5. the office of Stone & Rock Co. _____

6. a guess of someone _____

7. the drawings of Sheila and Ryan _____

8. food for the cats _____

9. plans of someone else _____

10. honks of the geese _____

14o   Use quotation marks to enclose a *direct quotation*—a person's exact words. A direct quotation always begins with a capital letter.

EXAMPLES   Sal said, **"H**elp me carry these books, guys.**"**
The president began, **"M**y fellow Americans. . . . **"**

Do not use quotation marks for an *indirect quotation.*

DIRECT QUOTATION   Nellie asked, "May I go?" [Nellie's exact words]
INDIRECT QUOTATION   Nellie asked if she could go. [not Nellie's exact words]

14p   When an expression such as *he said* divides a quoted sentence into two parts, the second part begins with a lowercase letter.

EXAMPLE   "I hope," Maria said**,** **"t**hat you remembered the binoculars."

If the second part of a divided quotation is a new sentence, a period (not a comma) follows the interrupting expression. The second part then begins with a capital letter.

EXAMPLE   "Tranh will come tomorrow," Hale said**.** **"H**e's taking his father to the airport."

NOTE   An interrupting expression is not part of a quotation, so it should never be located inside the quotation marks.

INCORRECT   "Kayla, Mom called, have you done your chores?"
CORRECT   "Kayla," Mom called, "have you done your chores?"

14q   Separate a direct quotation from the rest of a sentence with a comma, a question mark, or an exclamation point. Only use a period if the quotation ends the sentence.

EXAMPLES   "If you want to help**,"** Jessie said, "you'll have to be quieter."
"Will you join me at the show**?"** Willis asked.
Kalisha said, "Let's practice that again**."**

14r   Always place commas and periods inside the closing quotation marks.

EXAMPLE   "No**,"** Nori said, "I've never acted before. But I know I'll be a good performer**."**

14s   Always place colons and semicolons outside the closing quotation marks.

EXAMPLE   Tai said, "We are really desperate"**;** somehow, they still hadn't found enough workers for the science fair.

14t   Place question marks and exclamation points inside the closing quotation marks only if the quotation is a question or an exclamation. Otherwise, place them outside the closing quotation marks.

EXAMPLES   "Who is the current prime minister of Canada?"
Sarah yelled, "Out!"
Did I hear you say, "Kendrick Lamar"?
Don't you tell me, "Later"!

14u   When writing *dialogue* (a conversation), begin a new paragraph each time the speaker changes, and enclose each speaker's words in quotation marks.

EXAMPLE   "Wow!" Max exclaimed. "You're so good at this game."
"Thanks!" replied Darius. "It took me hours of practice."
Max suggested, "You could make a video showing some tips for playing it."
"Maybe," Darius pondered, "but only after I finish my homework."

14v   Use single quotation marks to enclose a quotation within a quotation.

EXAMPLES   Leonard said, "Don't forget that you said, 'Leonard, I promise to take you to the library when we're finished here.'" [Notice that the period is placed inside the single quotation mark.]
"What does he mean by saying, 'Last name first, first name, middle initial'?" Nadia asked. [Notice that the question mark is placed inside the double quotation marks, not the single quotation marks, because the words in the single quotation marks do not ask a question.]

14w   Use quotation marks to enclose titles of short works, such as short stories, short poems, essays, articles, songs, chapters and other parts of books, and individual TV, radio, and podcast episodes.

Type of Title	Examples
Short Stories	"Mother and Daughter"
Short Poems	"The Highwayman"
Essays	"Dream Children"
Articles	"Driver's Ed"
Songs	"Unforgettable"
TV, Radio, and Podcast Episodes	"The Confidence Mystery" "The Cataclysm Sentence"
Parts of Books	"Speaking and Listening Workshop"

EXERCISE 6 Correcting Sentences with Quotation Marks and Other Punctuation

In the sentences below, add quotation marks and other marks of punctuation where needed.

EX. I have trouble understanding trigonometry Josh said.
"I have trouble understanding trigonometry," Josh said.

1. Our teacher read us Bacon's essay entitled Gardens.

2. Coach, said Adrian please explain your strategy once more

3. The referee yelled Break it up

4. The firefighter came on the radio and asked Where's the fire

5. Did Luna really say The dog ate my homework

6. Stop asking questions yelled Ms. Stamos, exasperated.

7. The artist said, The sunshine is beautiful; it is reflecting magically off the water.

8. Let me come begged Joe, and I will help with the work—and the food!

9. Surely you are joking said the principal sternly

10. Kichi said, My favorite poem is My Mother Pieced Quilts.

EXERCISE 7 Proofreading Sentences

In the sentences below, add quotation marks and other marks of punctuation where needed. If a sentence is correct, write *C* above it.

EX. Let me practice my speech for you she said
"Let me practice my speech for you," she said.

1. The announcer said I asked Nathan Chen What's the most important skill for

    a skater

2. The title of this story, The Moustache, really interests me.

3. Rene, come here quickly yelled Magda. The birds are building a nest.

4. The pirate growled Tell me the secret

5. Did your grandmother always say to you, Eat your vegetables!

6. Buying a raffle ticket, Diego said Sometimes you win; but I responded, "Not very often.

7. Tammy's best friend Hilda asked her What did you mean when you told Guido Hilda's getting to be a pest

8. This is serious said our mother, and I will not tolerate any joking.

9. The clerk inquired, What's your name

10. Who's that hiding behind the chair asked the little girl

11. Was it James Hurst asked Matti who wrote The Scarlet Ibis?

12. What would you think about a song called Don't Worry, Be Happy?

13. Julio declared that lacrosse was his game.

14. Well drawled the impersonator, who do you think I'm supposed to be

15. Excuse me she said, clearing her throat. Is there any chance you could supply us with menus?

MODULE REVIEW

A. Correcting Sentences by Adding Punctuation Marks

In each of the sentences below, add the correct punctuation where needed. If a sentence is correct, write *C* above it.

EX. **"**The parade is rescheduled for next Saturday,**"** said the mayor**.**

1. Is that James' or the Joneses rake?

2. I think this is its best machine yet.

3. Does everyones lunch have a raw vegetable and a piece of fruit?

4. The Bureau of Indian Affairs news release was important.

5. "So . . ," the questioner began, "you say you did not arrive until 7:12 p.m

6. To decide whether to write a or an, think about the way in which the next word is spelled and pronounced.

7. The artistry of The Persistence of Memory is not only in the painting but also in the name.

8. At a museum we saw a life-size replica of the Spirit of St. Louis, Charles nicknamed "Lucky" Lindbergh's famous airplane.

9. How many u's are in vacuum?

10. Hey Corinne asked Why did that man name his boat Elvis

B. Proofreading a Paragraph for Errors in Punctuation

Working with a partner, use proofreading marks to correct the punctuation errors in the following summary of a classic sociology study.

EX. The book <u>Youth: Transition to Adulthood</u> was published in 1974.

[1] James S Coleman, a sociologist from the University of Chicago, chaired the Panel on Youth, which wrote this book. [2] The panel asked itself an enormous question How are young people brought into adulthood in the U S [3] In an agricultural society, children work with adults one can see examples in Little House on the Prairie and many other books. [4] With industrialization, children have become more isolated from family for work, being done mostly in the city, is isolated from family life. [5] Children do

not learn as often the work of their parents childrens futures are no longer determined by their parents occupations. [6] A striking fact of modern times is that, besides their parents and teachers, children have less contact with adults. [7] The group feels age segregation had its benefits it freed adults to work more efficiently and protected children from dangerous workplaces.

[8] However, children now have less opportunity to learn what adult life is like adults have less opportunity to enjoy being with children there is less sharing of activities less discussion and consequently less understanding between generations. [9] The panel suggested that the costs of age segregation see chart are higher than the benefits. [10] They suggest we ask if schools are the only places in which young people can learn to work their answer is No

C. Writing an Announcement

Your class is sponsoring a fund-raising event. You have been chosen by the class president to write an announcement to promote the event, which will be published on a community website. Decide what information to include in your announcement by answering the *5W-How?* Questions (*Who, When, Where, What, Why,* and *How*). Then write an announcement ten sentences long. Use at least three types of punctuation marks discussed in this module.

EX.   *Announcing the International Food Festival!*

Come to Fulton High School cafeteria on Saturday, May 10, at 10:00 A.M.

_____

_____

_____

_____

_____

_____

_____

_____

_____

_____

A dictionary entry is divided into several parts. Study the parts of the following sample dictionary entry.

```
          1      2      3    4              5
     cop•y (kŏp'ē), n., pl. cop'ies [Middle English < copie;
                               5                        6
     Medieval Latin < copia; Latin cōpia, plenty] 1. a thing
                               6
     made just like another; an imitation; a reproduction
              7                    8
     [a copy of the original] 2. [Now Rare] a model to be

     imitated, as of penmanship 3. any of a number of

     items, e.g., books or magazines, printed from identical
                                          3      4
     plates [a copy of the March issue] —vt., vi. cop'ied,
         4
     cop'y•ing 1. to make one or more copies of;

     reproduce; transcribe [copy a page] 2. to imitate [copy
                                9
     his gestures] —copy•ist, n.
                         10
     SYN. reproduction, duplicate ANT. original
```

1. **Entry word.** The entry word shows the correct spelling of a word. An alternate spelling may also be shown. The entry word shows how the word should be divided into syllables and may also show whether the word should be capitalized.

2. **Pronunciation.** The pronunciation is shown using accent marks, phonetic symbols, and diacritical marks. Every dictionary provides a guide to the symbols and marks it uses. Many online dictionaries feature audio to hear the correct pronunciation of a word.

3. **Part-of-speech labels.** These labels are usually abbreviated and show how the entry word should be used in a sentence. A word may be used as more than one part of speech. In such cases, a part-of-speech label is given before the set of definitions that matches each label.

4. **Other forms.** Sometimes a dictionary shows principal parts of verbs, spellings of plural forms of nouns, or the comparative forms of adjectives and adverbs.

5. **Etymology.** The *etymology* tells how a word or its parts entered the English language. It also shows how the word has changed over time.
6. **Definitions.** If the word has more than one meaning, its definitions are numbered or lettered.
7. **Sample usage.** Some dictionaries include sample phrases to illustrate particular meanings of words.
8. **Special usage labels.** These labels identify how a word is used (*Slang*), how common a word is (*Rare*), or how a word is used in a special field, such as botany (*Bot.*).
9. **Related word forms.** These are forms of the entry word created by adding suffixes or prefixes. Sometimes dictionaries also list common phrases in which the word appears.
10. **Synonyms and antonyms.** Words similar in meaning are ***synonyms.*** Words opposite in meaning are ***antonyms.*** Many dictionaries list synonyms and antonyms at the end of some word entries.

EXERCISE 1   Using a Dictionary

Use a dictionary to answer the questions below.

EX.   How many syllables are in the word *provincial*? _____ *three* _____

1. How is the word *momentarily* divided into syllables? _____
2. What is the spelling for the plural form of *potato*? _____
3. What are three different meanings for the word *pound*? _____

_____

4. What is the past tense of *defy*? _____
5. What is the etymology of the word *muckraker*? _____

_____

EXERCISE 2   Writing Words with Alternate Spellings

For each of the words below, write the alternate spelling on the line after the word.

EX.   disc _disk_

1. theater   _____   4. archaeology _____
2. valor   _____   5. catalog   _____
3. judgment   _____

SPELLING RULES

---

ie and ei

15a   Write *ie* when the sound is long *e*, except after *c*.

EXAMPLES   believe, piece, field, receive, conceit, perceive

EXCEPTIONS   weird, either, seize, leisure, neither, species

15b   Write *ei* when the sound is not long *e*, especially when the sound is long *a*.

EXAMPLES   freight, weigh, veil, heir, forfeit

EXCEPTIONS   mischief, conscience, view, friend, science, pie

-cede, -ceed, and -sede

15c   The only English word ending in *-sede* is *supersede*. The only words ending in *-ceed* are *exceed*, *proceed*, and *succeed*. All other words with this sound end in *-cede*.

EXAMPLES   accede, concede, recede, precede, intercede, secede

---

EXERCISE 3   Writing Words with *ie* and *ei*

Fill in the blank in each word below with the letters *ie* or *ei* to spell the word correctly. Use a dictionary as needed.

EX.   ach __*ie*__ ve

1. rec _____ pt
2. p _____ ce
3. gr _____ f
4. handkerch _____ f
5. n _____ ce
6. p _____ r
7. f _____ ld
8. s _____ zed
9. br _____ f

10. th _____ r
11. f _____ rce
12. fr _____ nd
13. f _____ gn
14. ch _____ f
15. b _____ ge
16. c _____ ling
17. n _____ ther
18. sl _____ gh

19. bel _____ f
20. pr _____ st
21. counterf _____ t
22. w _____ rd
23. sh _____ ld
24. r _____ ndeer
25. y _____ ld

EXERCISE 4   Proofreading a Paragraph to Correct Spelling Errors

The paragraphs below contain ten spelling errors. Underline the misspelled words, and write the correct spelling above each misspelled word. If a sentence is correct, write *C* above it. Use a dictionary as needed.

received

EX.   For first prize in the science fair, I <u>recieved</u> tickets to go whale watching.

[1] Whale watching is something my freind Jake and I had always wanted to do, so I proceded to sign us up for the first available trip. [2] As we left the harbor and the land receeded from veiw, all the passengers on the whale-watching boat grew excited. [3] Two sceintists who study whales were on board. [4] They provided interesting information, and they also interceeded in discussions. [5] For example, two people got into an argument about which were larger, modern whales or the anceint dinosaurs.

[6] The scientists said that this year they were seeing fewer whales. [7] The preceeding day, they had spotted only one humpback whale, but this day they were hoping to see more. [8] The passengers acceeded to the scientists' request that we scan the horizon for whales. [9] After only ten minutes, something happened that I could not beleive. [10] The water rippled, and a giant humpback leaped out of the water.

PREFIXES AND SUFFIXES

A *prefix* is a letter or a group of letters added to the beginning of a word to change its meaning.

15d   When adding a prefix to a word, do not change the spelling of the word itself.

EXAMPLES   re + assure = **re**assure   super + human = **super**human
            un + tie = **un**tie   under + sea = **under**sea
            il + legal = **il**legal   over + rate = **over**rate

A *suffix* is a letter or a group of letters added to the end of a word to change its meaning.

15e   When adding the suffix -*ness* or -*ly* to a word, the spelling of the original word usually remains the same.

EXAMPLES   lean + ness = lean**ness**   great + ness = great**ness**
            glad + ly = glad**ly**   habitual + ly = habitual**ly**

NOTE   For most words that end in *y*, change the *y* to *i* before adding -*ly* or -*ness*.

        EXAMPLES   ordinary + ly = ordinar**ily**   happy + ly = happ**ily**
                    empty + ness = empt**iness**   bossy + ness = boss**iness**

15f   Drop the final silent *e* before a suffix beginning with a vowel.

EXAMPLES   use + able = us**able**   create + ive = creat**ive**
            write + er = writ**er**   amaze + ing = amaz**ing**

EXCEPTION   Keep the silent *e* in words ending in *ce* and *ge* before a suffix beginning with *a* or *o*.

            EXAMPLES   peace + able = peac**eable**   courage + ous = courag**eous**

EXCEPTION   Keep the final silent *e* in instances where dropping it would cause confusion.

            EXAMPLES   dy**ei**ng (to avoid confusion with *dying*)
                        sing**ei**ng (to avoid confusion with *singing*)

15g   Keep the final silent *e* before a suffix beginning with a consonant.

EXAMPLES   fate + ful = fat**eful**   noise + less = nois**eless**
            late +ly = lat**ely**   awe + some + aw**esome**

EXCEPTIONS   argue + ment = argu**ment**   true + ly = tru**ly**
              judge + ment = judg**ment**   nine+ th = nin**th**

EXERCISE 5   Spelling Words with Prefixes and Suffixes

On each line below, add the given prefix or suffix to the word. Use a dictionary as needed.

EX.   re + arrange _rearrange_

1. un + do _____

2. kind + ness _____

3. re + make _____

4. become + ing _____

5. un + intentional _____

6. wise + ly _____

7. mile + age _____

8. im + mortal _____

9. sure + ly _____

10. il + logical _____

11. open + ness _____

12. notice + able _____

13. merry + ly _____

14. re + discover _____

15. advantage + ous _____

16. dis + appoint _____

17. final + ly _____

18. store + ed _____

19. im + material _____

20. dense + ly _____

EXERCISE 6   Spelling Words with Suffixes

On each line below, add the given suffix to the word. Use a dictionary as needed.

EX.   silly + ness _silliness_

1. mediate + or _____

2. judge + ment _____

3. brave + ly _____

4. care + ful _____

5. active + ity _____

6. practical + ly _____

7. outrage + ous _____

8. heavy + ness _____

9. time + less _____

10. real + ly _____

11. dose + age _____

12. busy + ly _____

13. cleanly + ness _____

14. continue + ous _____

15. merry + ly _____

16. moderate + ion _____

17. interesting + ly _____

18. note + able _____

19. hopeful + ly _____

20. fascinate + ion _____

15h For words ending in *y* preceded by a consonant, change the *y* to *i* before any suffix that does not begin with *i*.

EXAMPLES   forty + eth = fort**ieth**   glory + ous = glor**ious**

                reply + ed = repl**ied**   rely + able = rel**iable**

EXCEPTIONS shy + ly = shy**ly**   sly + ness = sly**ness**

15i For words ending in *y* preceded by a vowel, keep the *y* when adding a suffix.

EXAMPLES   play + ful = play**ful**   array + ed = array**ed**

EXCEPTIONS lay + ed = la**id**   day + ly = da**ily**

15j Double the final consonant before adding a suffix that begins with a vowel if the word (1) has only one syllable or has the accent on the final syllable and (2) ends in a single consonant preceded by a single vowel.

EXAMPLES   run + er = run**ner**   grab + ed = gra**bbed**

                sit + ing = si**tting**   big + est = bi**ggest**

Do not double the final consonant unless the word satisfies both of the conditions.

EXAMPLES   near + est = nearest   feel + ing = feeling

                clean + er = cleaner   fear + ed = feared

EXERCISE 7   Spelling Words with Suffixes

In the space above each item, add the given suffix to the word.

EX. fly + ing *flying*

1. cook + ing

2. funny + er

3. bat + ed

4. marry + ing

5. treat + ed

6. near + est

7. joy + ful

8. fair + est

9. ship + ed

10. put + ing

EXERCISE 8   Proofreading to Correct Spelling in a Composition

In the paragraphs below, underline the twenty spelling errors. Write the correct spelling above each misspelled word. If a sentence is correct, write *C* above it. Use a dictionary as needed.

studying
EX.   We have been <u>studiing</u> the legend of Atlantis, the lost continent.

[1] Ordinaryly, I am not very interested in science fiction or mythology, but this story fascinates me. [2] Atlantis, some people believe, was a mysteryous continent that existed thousands of years ago. [3] No one is exactly sure of the beginings of the Atlantis story. [4] However, varyous ancient accounts describe Atlantis and how it vanished. [5] The Greek philosopher Plato told a story about a beautyful island that existed in the Atlantic Ocean long before his time. [6] He described great cities and people living in prosperity and happyness on this island. [7] Then an earthquake occured. [8] The earthquake destroied the island, and it sank beneath the sea.

[9] An extraordinaryly popular account of the Atlantis story was written by Ignatius Donnelly and published in 1882. [10] He believed that the first people in Europe, Asia, and the Americas were colonists who had sailled from Atlantis. [11] Donnelly portraied their gloryous, lost civilization.

[12] Jules Verne creatted his own version of Atlantis in his novel *Twenty Thousand Leagues Under the Sea.* [13] The novel tells of the adventures of Captain Nemo and his submarine. One scene describes a visit to Atlantis.

[14] Other writers have called the lost continent Lemuria and have located it nearrer to Asia than to Europe. [15] A retired British army officer wrote four books in which he tryed to persuade people that there had been a lost civilization called Lemuria, or Mu. [16] He claimmed he had seen tablets written by the people of Mu. [17] According to his story, the tablets were kept in monasterys in India.

[18] Did the lost continent really exist, and is it today traped beneath the ocean? [19] You might think that this idea is terrifiing or impossible.

[20] There is no deniing, however, that the idea is intriguing.

MODULE 15: SPELLING
PLURALS OF NOUNS

15k   **Form the plurals of most nouns by adding *-s*.**

SINGULAR   car   tree   radio   tent   president
  PLURAL   cars   trees   radios   tents   presidents

15l   **Form the plurals of nouns ending in *s, x, z, ch,* or *sh* by adding *-es*.**

SINGULAR   beach   blintz   fox   bush   mess
  PLURAL   beaches   blintzes   foxes   bushes   messes

NOTE   Proper nouns usually follow these rules, too.

EXAMPLES   Ericksons   Navarros
           Davises   Lopezes

EXERCISE 9   Spelling the Plurals of Nouns

On the line after each noun, write the correct plural form.

EX.   stitch   *stitches*

1. waltz   _____
2. valley   _____
3. dime   _____
4. Forster   _____
5. mountain   _____
6. song   _____
7. radish   _____
8. glass   _____
9. Martinez   _____
10. turtle   _____
11. lunch   _____
12. wish   _____
13. idea   _____

14. box   _____
15. Katz   _____
16. dancer   _____
17. Morrison   _____
18. watch   _____
19. inventor   _____
20. dish   _____
21. dress   _____
22. Ross   _____
23. fizz   _____
24. benefit   _____
25. march   _____

15m   Form the plurals of nouns ending in *y* preceded by a consonant by changing the *y* to *i* and adding *-es.*

SINGULAR	story	sky	theory	city	party
	stor**ies**	sk**ies**	theor**ies**	cit**ies**	part**ies**

EXCEPTION   With proper nouns, simply add *-s.*

EXAMPLES   the Chomsky**s**, the Kerry**s**

15n   Form the plurals of nouns ending in *y* preceded by a vowel by adding *-s.*

SINGULAR	boy	tray	turkey	Monday	convoy
PLURAL	boy**s**	tray**s**	turkey**s**	Monday**s**	convoy**s**

15o   Form the plurals of most nouns ending in *f* by adding *-s.* The plurals of some nouns ending in *f* or *-fe* are formed by changing the *f* to *v* and adding *-es.*

SINGULAR	staff	roof	cliff	leaf	elf	wife
PLURAL	staff**s**	roof**s**	cliff**s**	lea**ves**	el**ves**	wi**ves**

NOTE   When you are not sure how to spell the plural of a noun ending in *f* or *fe,* check the spelling in a dictionary.

EXERCISE 10   Spelling the Plurals of Nouns

On the line after each noun, write the correct plural form. Use a dictionary as needed.

EX.   belief *beliefs*

1. wolf _____
2. Tuesday _____
3. essay _____
4. carafe _____
5. trophy _____
6. Kelly _____
7. enemy _____
8. knife _____
9. life _____
10. penny _____

11. laundry _____
12. lamp _____
13. wharf _____
14. monkey _____
15. chief _____
16. Hardy _____
17. baby _____
18. reef _____
19. journey _____
20. folly _____

15p Form the plurals of nouns ending in *o* preceded by a vowel by adding *-s*. Form the plurals of many nouns ending in *o* preceded by a consonant by adding *-es*.

SINGULAR	patio	stereo	veto	potato	tomato
PLURAL	patio**s**	stereo**s**	veto**es**	potato**es**	tomato**es**

EXCEPTIONS	silo**s**	photo**s**	burrito**s**

Form the plurals of most musical terms ending in *o* by adding *–s*.

SINGULAR	piano	concerto	solo	oratorio
PLURAL	piano**s**	concerto**s**	solo**s**	oratorio**s**

NOTE To form the plurals of some nouns ending in *o* preceded by a consonant, you may add either *-s* or *-es*.

SINGULAR	grotto	mosquito	cargo
PLURAL	grotto**s**	mosquito**s**	cargo**s**
	or	*or*	*or*
	grotto**es**	mosquito**es**	cargo**es**

NOTE When you are not sure how to spell the plural of a noun ending in *o*, check the spelling in a dictionary.

15q The plurals of a few nouns are formed in an irregular manner.

SINGULAR	mouse	ox	man	goose	foot
PLURAL	m**ice**	ox**en**	m**en**	g**ee**se	f**ee**t

15r Form the plural of a compound noun consisting of a noun plus a modifier by making the modified noun plural.

SINGULAR	attorney-at-law	passerby	editor in chief	blueprint
PLURAL	attorney**s**-at-law	passer**s**by	editor**s** in chief	blueprint**s**

EXERCISE 11   Spelling the Plurals of Nouns

On the line after each noun, write its correct plural form. Use a dictionary as needed.

EX. solo *solos*

1. rodeo _____
2. volcano _____
3. soprano _____
4. radio _____
5. cello _____

6. person _____
7. yard sale _____
8. father-in-law _____
9. hairdo _____
10. runner-up _____

EXERCISE 12   Proofreading to Correct Spelling Errors in Sentences

In the sentences below, underline the spelling errors. Write the correct spelling above each misspelled word. If a sentence is correct, write *C* above it. Use a dictionary as needed.

children
EX.   All the <u>childs</u> in the Kelly family enjoy playing music.

1. Two rooms in their house are used as music studioes.

2. Passerbys often pause to listen to Cara and her brother when they play their pianos.

3. Cara has played concertoes and other symphonic pieces with the local symphony orchestra.

4. Cara says that most of her heros are musicians.

5. I have seen photoes in the newspaper of Cara's sister and mother, who perform together.

6. They are both sopranoes and love to sing opera.

7. Both of Cara's sisters-in-laws have become interested in music.

8. The family made a recording, and discs jockeys in our town often play selections from it.

9. Each year, the Kellys perform soloes at a concert in our town.

10. This concert is so popular that even the threat of tornadoes wouldn't keep people from coming to it.

EXERCISE 13   Using Plurals Correctly

Write a sentence for each word below, using that word's plural form. Use a dictionary as needed.

EX.   notary public   <u>*All three notaries public will certify documents for free.*</u>

1. looker-on _____

2. foot _____

3. piano _____

4. mosquito _____

5. echo _____

6. burrito _____

7. pueblo _____

8. goose _____

9. halo _____

10. two-year-old _____

A.   Correcting Spelling Errors in Sentences

Underline all misspelled words in each sentence below. Then write the words correctly above each misspelled word.

tomatoes
EX.   This recipe calls for green <u>tomatos</u>.

1. Volunteers worked all day preparing releif packages for the victims of the storm.

2. Every year, my nephew looks forward to the leafs changing when fall arrives.

3. My mother is always saying, "If at first you don't sucede, try again."

4. After the second-string quarterback scored three touchdowns, the announcers agreed that they had underated his abilities.

5. The pharmacist wrote down the correct doseage for the medicine.

6. Although it was late and they were tired, the campers sat around their campfire, singing merryly.

7. Do you know which president preceeded Lincoln?

8. Cho Yia's couragous act was highly praised.

9. My favorite poems have a timless quality to them.

10. Fortunately, Lian had remembered to bring along a magnifiing glass.

11. I find my new daily planner very usful.

12. The coollest spot in the yard was under the old oak tree.

13. When the famous bater stepped up to the plate, the crowd roared in anticipation.

14. In this area of South America, the visitors found many ranchs and farms.

15. Rosa dropped her keyes in the snow, and it took quite a while to find them.

16. Maya Santiago is new to my school, and the Santiagoes have invited several families in the neighborhood to a block party this Saturday.

17. The class made a study of the varieties of fish found in corals reefs.

18. Andrea is doing a report about the lifes of famous politicians.

19. The ceremonys have been repeated every year.

20. As we called from the rim of the canyon, our echos filled the air.

B. Proofreading a Paragraph to Correct Spelling Errors

Underline the misspelled words in paragraph below, and write the correct spelling above each misspelled word. Some sentences may contain more than one error. Use a dictionary as needed.

stories

EX.   The history of mountaineering is filled with <u>storys</u> of adventure.

[1] Some people beleive that mountaineering began in 218 BCE when Hannibal crossed the Alps with nine thousand soldier and thirty-seven elephants. [2] Another early mountain-climbing feat occured in 126 CE, when Emperor Hadrian scalled Mt. Etna, in Italy, to see a sunrise. [3] The sport of mountaineering really had its begining, however, in the 1800s, when people tryed to climb the great peaks of the Alps. [4] Between 1854 and 1865, climbers suceded in reaching the summits of 180 previously unclimbed Alpine mountains. [5] Another range of mountains that began to recieve attention from mountaineers at this time was the Himalayas, the tallest mountains in the world. [6] One of the great mysterys of mountaineering is the story of George Mallory and Andrew Irvine, who tried to climb the world's highest mountain, Mt. Everest, in 1924. [7] They disappeared as they were nearring the summit, and no one knows if they actually reached the top. [8] That acheivement was accomplished officially in 1953 by Edmund Hillary and Sherpa Tenzing Norgay. [9] No matter how carefully climbers plan their ascent, they are still at the mercy of sudden changes in the weather. [10] But the thrill of reaching one of the highest places in the world seems to make up for the riskes these climbers take.

C. Creating a Spelling Lesson

You have volunteered to help tutor elementary students. Your task is to help them understand the rules of English spelling. Choose two of the spelling rules from this module to present to your students. Write each rule and provide examples. Then, for each rule, make up an exercise that contains at least five items. List the answers in parentheses.

EX.   *RULE: Write ie when the sound is long e, except after c.*

EXAMPLES: achieve, receive, brief, ceiling

EXERCISE 1 Spelling Words with ie and ei

On the line in each word, write ie or ei to spell the word correctly.

EX. s ei ze

_____

_____

_____

_____

_____

_____

_____

_____

_____

_____

_____

_____

_____

_____

_____

_____

_____

_____

_____

_____

_____